REVELATIONS FROM
A 45-POUND PURSE

REVELATIONS FROM A 45-POUND PURSE

A  Collection

by Cathy Guisewite

Andrews and McMeel
A Universal Press Syndicate Company
Kansas City

5

WHO'S HANDLING THE BAKER DEAL, CATHY?

NO ONE. NEXT MONDAY'S A HOLIDAY SO EVERYONE'S PLANNING TO SNEAK OUT EARLY ON FRIDAY.

SINCE WE KNOW WE'RE LEAVING EARLY ON FRIDAY, WE'LL BE USELESS ON THURSDAY, DISTRACTED ON WEDNESDAY AND RESTLESS ALL DAY TOMORROW.

BASICALLY, ALL REAL WORK STOPPED AT 9:15 THIS MORNING AND WON'T RESUME UNTIL SEPTEMBER 8!

IT TAKES A RESOURCEFUL TEAM TO TURN A ONE-DAY HOLIDAY INTO A TWO-WEEK VACATION...

WHAT DO YOU WANT TO DO FOR LUNCH, CATHY?

I WANT MY MOTHER TO BRING ME A NICE HOT PLATE OF FOOD.

I WANT HER TO SIT HERE AND TELL ME HOW WONDERFUL I AM WHILE I EAT IT, AND WHEN I'M FINISHED I WANT HER TO KISS ME ON THE CHEEK AND TELL ME TO RUN OFF AND PLAY!!

CATHY HAS STARED AT THE CARRY-OUT MENUS ONE TOO MANY TIMES.

I'LL RENT THIS MOVIE AND HAVE A NICE, QUIET EVENING BY MYSELF...

VIDEO-RENT
ROMANCE
ACTION
COMEDY
HORROR

I'LL GET THIS ONE IN CASE IRVING COMES OVER...I'LL GET THIS ONE IN CASE HE COMES OVER AND HAS ALREADY SEEN THE OTHER ONE...I'LL GET THIS ONE IN CASE HE DOESN'T COME OVER AND I DON'T LIKE WHAT I GOT FOR MYSELF...

I'LL GET THIS ONE IN CASE HE DOES COME OVER, WE HATE ALL THE OTHER ONES AND NEED A BACKUP...I'LL GET THIS ONE AS A BACKUP TO THE BACKUP ...THIS ONE AS A BACKUP TO THE BACKUP TO THE BACKUP...

ARE YOU A MEMBER?

LET'S JUST SAY I'M ON THE CONTINGENCY PLAN.

POP

6

ZENITH IS HIGHLY ADVANCED IN COGNITIVE SKILLS AND THE LINKING OF EMOTIONAL IDEAS TO CREATE COMPLEX INTERACTIONS.

"SHE THROWS TEMPER TANTRUMS."

AS SHE MOVES INTO THIS SCARY NEW GROWTH ARENA, SHE'S CHOSEN TO SUPPRESS HER FORMERLY BRILLIANT VERBAL SKILLS IN LIEU OF COMPLEX GESTURING AND SPACIAL PLAY!

"SHE SCREAMS INSTEAD OF TALKING."

AS HER DAYTIME CAREGIVERS, I KNOW YOU'LL TREASURE AND NURTURE THIS EXCITING PHASE JUST AS HER DADDY AND I DO!

"BOLT THE CUPBOARDS AND DON THE RAIN GEAR!!"

AMAZING.

I KNOW! SHE'S VERY QUICK FOR A 60-YEAR-OLD!

ZENITH, NO! WHAT ARE YOU DOING?? YOU NEVER DO THAT AT HOME!!

SHE NEVER DOES THAT AT HOME!

I DON'T KNOW WHERE SHE LEARNED THAT! SHE'S NEVER DONE ANYTHING EVEN REMOTELY LIKE THAT BEFORE!!

RIGHT ON SCHEDULE. THIRTY MONTHS AFTER GIVING BIRTH, THE DENIAL HORMONE KICKS IN.

"OPEN A LITTLE BOUTIQUE", I SAID... BUT NO. YOU DIDN'T WANT THE INVENTORY HASSLE.

"GET A NICE OFFICE JOB," I SAID... BUT NO. YOU DIDN'T WANT TO BE TIED TO SOME CORPORATE ROUTINE.

"INVITE EIGHT PRESCHOOL HOODLUMS TO SHOW UP AT 7:30 AND RAMPAGE MY HOME UNTIL 6 P.M."... YOU LOVED IT!! YOU HAD TO DO IT!!

FLO ALWAYS GETS CRANKY WHEN SHE MISSES HER AFTERNOON NAP.

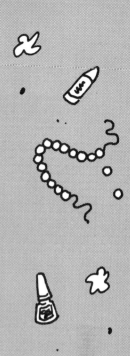

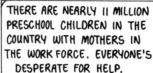

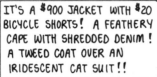

Panel 1: FALL DRESSING '91! THE MOOD IS WILD AND THE BUZZWORD IS WACKY!

Panel 2: IT'S A $900 JACKET WITH $20 BICYCLE SHORTS! A FEATHERY CAPE WITH SHREDDED DENIM! A TWEED COAT OVER AN IRIDESCENT CAT SUIT!!

Panel 3: IT'S ELEGANCE WITH AN AIR OF IRREVERENCE... TRADITION WITH AN AIR OF FUNK...COUTURE WITH AN AIR OF CAMP!

Panel 4: SALESCLERKS WITH AN AIR OF DESPERATION.

DID YOU WANT THAT??

Panel 5: I'M TOO SHORT AND DUMPY TO WEAR A PLAID SUIT.

OF COURSE YOU LOOK SHORT AND DUMPY IF YOU JUST **STAND** THERE!

Panel 6: DON'T YOU PEOPLE READ THE FASHION ADS?? YOU HAVE TO **MOVE**!! TOSS YOUR HEAD BACK! KICK UP YOUR HEELS! ROMP THROUGH TRAFFIC JAMS CLUTCHING FLORAL BOUQUETS AND WAVING AT HANDSOME YOUNG MEN! A BLUR OF COLOR! BUT YOU HAVE TO **MOVE**!! **MOVE**!!

Panel 7:

Panel 8: WE HAVE AN ATTITUDE PROBLEM IN DRESSING ROOM NUMBER 2.

Panel 9: FOR THE OFFICE, A NUBBY-TWEED ENGLISH RIDING OUTFIT!

Panel 10: FOR DINNER PARTIES, A DIVER-INSPIRED SCUBA DRESS!

Panel 11: FOR MOVIE DATES, SKI PANTS AND APRÉS SKI BOOTS!

Panel 12: EXHAUSTED FROM A DAY OF TRYING ON "ACTIVE WEAR," THE '90s WOMAN DRIVES HOME AND TAKES A NAP IN HER WORKOUT CLOTHES.

BRAND-NEW PANTS...PERFECT, BUT I CAN'T WEAR THEM UNTIL THE LEGS ARE SHORTENED...

BRAND-NEW SUIT... PERFECT, BUT I CAN'T WEAR IT UNTIL THE SLEEVES AND SKIRT ARE SHORTENED...

THAT DOES IT! I SHOPPED. I BOUGHT. I TRIED. I AM NOT WEARING MY SAME, TIRED OLD CLOTHES JUST BECAUSE EVERY NEW THING NEEDS TO BE SHORTENED!!!

SWEATSUIT WITH CHARGE CARD RECEIPTS STAPLED TO IT. VERY INTERESTING.

IT'S MY NEW FALL LOOK: "FASHION PENDING."

MY ROMANCE IS PERFECT... THEN MY ROMANCE IS HIDEOUS... THEN MY ROMANCE IS PERFECT... THEN MY ROMANCE IS HIDEOUS...

I LOVE MY JOB... THEN I HATE MY JOB... THEN I LOVE MY JOB... THEN I HATE MY JOB...

I'M THRIFTY... THEN I SPEND TOO MUCH... THEN I'M THRIFTY... THEN I SPEND TOO MUCH...

HAVING REACHED A WEIGHT PLATEAU FROM WHICH I CAN'T BUDGE, I'VE NOW TRANSFERRED THE CONCEPT OF "YO-YO DIETING" TO EVERY OTHER AREA OF MY LIFE.

I HAD A GREAT TIME TONIGHT, CATHY!

"GREAT??" REALLY? YOU NEVER SAY THAT, IRVING.

I DID. I HAD A GREAT TIME.

WHY WAS IT MORE GREAT THAN OTHER TIMES?

IT WAS JUST GREAT.

BUT GREAT IN WHAT WAY??

IT WAS GREAT, OK?? I HAD A GREAT TIME!!

THRILLED, YET TERRIFIED BY A HINT OF NEW CLOSENESS, SHE FLINGS THE RELATIONSHIP BACK INTO THE STATUS QUO...

BUT WHAT, SPECIFICALLY, WAS GREAT??

15

YOU SPENT $150 ON A NEW GOLF CLUB??

SO WHAT? YOU PROBABLY SPENT $150 ON THAT NEW SWEATER.

I ONLY BOUGHT THIS SWEATER TO LOOK BEAUTIFUL FOR YOU. THAT'S A WHOLE DIFFERENT THING, IRVING.

WHEN I SPEND MONEY, IT'S BECAUSE I'M THINKING OF YOU! WHEN YOU SPEND MONEY, IT'S BECAUSE YOU'RE THINKING OF YOU! ALL THE MONEY IS GOING TO YOU!

MY GIRLFRIEND: MASTER OF THE REVOLVING GUILT ACCOUNT.

APPROPRIATE USES FOR $50

HIM:	HER:
* HAVE CAR DETAILED	* HAVE FACIAL
* WORLD SERIES TICKET	* THEATER TICKET
* RADAR DETECTOR	* PSYCHIC READING
* 40 GOLF BALLS	* HALF A BLOUSE
* BOTTLE OF FINE WINE	* 150 CANS OF DIET SODA
* YEAR'S SUPPLY OF UNDERWEAR	* ONE PIECE OF LINGERIE

((RIP RIP))
((WAD WAD))
((RIP))

* EIGHT HOURS AT THE DRIVING RANGE.

* ONE HOUR WITH THE THERAPIST.

HOW MUCH DO YOU HAVE IN YOUR SAVINGS ACCOUNT, CHARLENE?

WHAT??

IRVING AND I HAVE BEEN FIGHTING ABOUT MONEY. I JUST WANT SOME PERSPECTIVE.

YOU CAN'T ASK PEOPLE ABOUT MONEY, CATHY!

MONEY IS TOO PERSONAL! TOO PRIVATE! HOO, BOY! NO! NO WAY! NO MONEY DISCUSSIONS!

NEVER MIND.

COME BACK WHEN YOU'RE FIGHTING ABOUT SEX!!

HI, IRVING, IT'S CATHY... ARE YOU BUSY?

NO.

I JUST WANTED TO SAY I'M SORRY ABOUT OUR FIGHT LAST NIGHT, AND TO WHISPER ALL THE LITTLE WAYS I WANT TO MAKE IT UP TO YOU TONIGHT... HEE, HEE...STARTING WITH...

UH, I HAVE SOME PEOPLE IN MY OFFICE RIGHT NOW.

PEOPLE?? AACK! I ASKED IF YOU WERE BUSY!! YOU DIDN'T SAY YOU HAD PEOPLE THERE!!

YOU DIDN'T ASK IF I HAD PEOPLE HERE.

DID YOU CALL IRVING AND SAY WHAT I TOLD YOU TO, CATHY? HOO, BOY! IT ALWAYS DRIVES SIMON WILD!!

IRVING SPENDS $300 ON SOME CAR GIZMO AND THEN SAYS I'M IRRESPONSIBLE ABOUT MONEY, MOM!

YOU'RE FIGHTING ABOUT MONEY??

THAT'S WHAT **MARRIED** PEOPLE FIGHT ABOUT! YOU'RE FIGHTING LIKE **MARRIED** PEOPLE!

WHEN PEOPLE START FIGHTING LIKE MARRIED PEOPLE, THEY'RE PREPARING TO **BE** MARRIED PEOPLE!! OH, **HAPPY DAY**!! OH, **HALLELUJAH**!! OUR BABY'S PREPARING TO BE A MARRIED PERSON!!!

SHE CAN WRING LIFE FROM A STONE, DAD.

SHE'S A MOTHER, HONEY.

YOU MADE DINNER, CATHY??

JUST PART OF MY COMMITMENT TO FRUGALITY, IRVING!

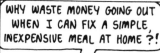

WHY WASTE MONEY GOING OUT WHEN I CAN FIX A SIMPLE, INEXPENSIVE MEAL AT HOME?!

...WHICH, WHEN YOU ADD THE INGREDIENTS, THE COOKBOOKS, THE NEW PANS, THE NEW SPICES, THE REPLACEMENT INGREDIENTS FOR THE ONES I RUINED, THE FOUR LONG-DISTANCE CALLS TO GIRLFRIENDS WHO KNOW HOW TO COOK AND THE DAY I TOOK OFF TO WORK TO DO IT, COMES TO $215 A SERVING.

WE SHOULD DO THIS MORE OFTEN!

YES!...SAY, JUNE OF 1998?

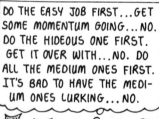

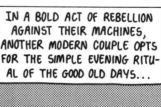

AS YOU KNOW, THIS OFFICE HAS ALWAYS PRIDED ITSELF ON ITS PROGRESSIVE ATTITUDE TOWARD WOMEN.

WHILE MOST COMPANIES RUSHED INTO DISCUSSIONS ABOUT SEXUAL HARASSMENT RIGHT AFTER THE THOMAS-HILL INCIDENT, I FELT WE ALL NEEDED A FEW WEEKS FOR PERSONAL REFLECTION.

BY WAITING UNTIL TODAY, I BELIEVE I'VE ONCE AGAIN DEMONSTRATED MY PROFOUND SENSITIVITY TO THE FEELINGS OF THE WOMEN IN OUR WORKPLACE...

...ACCORDING TO MY WALL CALENDAR, THE MAJORITY OF YOU ARE NOW SAFELY PAST YOUR P.M.S. DAYS!

I WAS SHOCKED TO HEAR OF SEXUAL HARASSMENT INCIDENTS IN OTHER COMPANIES.

I WAS APPALLED TO THINK ANY MAN COULD BE OBLIVIOUS TO HIS OWN OBNOXIOUS BEHAVIOR, AND I WAS SICKENED TO THINK ANY WOMAN WOULDN'T FEEL FREE TO SPEAK UP!

IF ANYONE HERE HAS EVER FELT OFFENDED BY ANYTHING I'VE EVER SAID OR DONE, I INVITE THEM TO COME FORWARD IMMEDIATELY!

...KEEPING IN MIND THAT HOLIDAY BONUS TIME IS RIGHT AROUND THE CORNER...

IF I HAVE TO TAKE DOWN MY CINDY CRAWFORD POSTER, YOU HAVE TO TAKE DOWN YOUR "HUNK-A-DAY" CALENDAR!

HAH! I'M NOT TAKING DOWN MY "HUNK-A-DAY" UNTIL YOU FORK OVER MY VICTORIA'S SECRET CATALOG!!

YOU CAN HAVE YOUR VICTORIA'S SECRET CATALOG WHEN I GET BACK MY SWIMSUIT ISSUE!

THE SWIMSUIT ISSUE GOES BACK WHEN I GET MY ROB LOWE VIDEO BACK!

HAH!

I THINK THE STAFF NEEDS A FEW WORDS FROM YOU, MR. PINKLEY.

NO ONE GETS THE ROB LOWE VIDEO BACK UNTIL MY X-RATED FAX FILE IS RETURNED!

27

EVER SINCE THE THOMAS-HILL FLAP, EMPLOYEE MORALE HAS BEEN IN THE TOILET, CATHY.

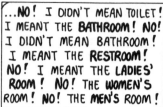

...NO! I DIDN'T MEAN TOILET! I MEANT THE **BATHROOM**! NO! I DIDN'T MEAN BATHROOM! I MEANT THE **RESTROOM**! NO! I MEANT THE **LADIES'** ROOM! NO! THE **WOMEN'S** ROOM! NO! THE **MEN'S** ROOM!

NO! THE **UNISEX** ROOM! NO! NOT UNISEX!! NO SEX! I DIDN'T MENTION SEX! I DIDN'T SAY **ANYTHING**! STRIKE THE RECORD! I AM INNOCENT!!

IT'S OK, MR. PINKLEY. WE'RE ALL KIND OF FLIRTING WITH DISASTER RIGHT NOW.

I WAS **NOT** FLIRTING! NO FLIRTING! THAT WASN'T FLIRTING!

TO HELP EXPLAIN SEXUAL HARASSMENT, WE'VE PREPARED A ROLE-PLAYING EXERCISE. CATHY WILL PRETEND TO BE THE POWERFUL MALE BOSS, AND FRED WILL BE THE SUBORDINATE FEMALE.

YOUR REPORT WAS FINE, FRED, BUT WHAT I'D REALLY LIKE TO GET MY HANDS ON IS THAT INCREDIBLE LITTLE TUSHIE!

YOU WOULD?? OKAY! NOW?? YES!!

I'M YOUR BOSS! YOUR CAREER DEPENDS ON MAINTAINING RESPECT!

I ALWAYS KNEW YOU HAD THE HOTS FOR ME!!

GET ME OUT OF HERE!

YES! TO THE COPY ROOM!

MR. PINKLEY!

OH, GOOD! CAN I GO NEXT?

WHERE'S MR. PINKLEY, CATHY?

SIX MORE WOMEN FILED SEXUAL HARASSMENT COMPLAINTS TODAY AND HE SORT OF SNAPPED.

HE'S BEEN LOCKED IN THE CONFERENCE ROOM ALL MORNING WITH THE KEY OFFENDERS.

I KNOW HE HOPED THE PROBLEM WOULD JUST DISAPPEAR, BUT WE HAVE FORMAL COMPLAINT PROCEDURES HE HAS TO FOLLOW NOW! HE'S FINALLY FORCED TO DEAL WITH IT IN A MATURE, RESPONSIBLE WAY!

CONFERENCE ROOM

THE MANAGEMENT SQUAD AND I ARE GOING ON A FIVE-DAY WARRIOR MALE-BONDING RETREAT!

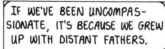

Panel 1:
HOW CAN YOU ACCEPT THE MEN IN THE OFFICE GOING ON A "WARRIOR RETREAT," CATHY?!

I UNDERSTAND, CHARLENE.

Panel 2:
YOU UNDERSTAND??

WELL, I DON'T REALLY UNDERSTAND HOW THE MEN FEEL, BUT I UNDERSTAND WHY I DON'T UNDERSTAND.

Panel 3:
...WELL, I DON'T TOTALLY UNDERSTAND WHY I DON'T UNDERSTAND, BUT I HAVE A VAGUE IDEA AS TO WHY IT'S PROBABLY NOT POSSIBLE TO EVER HAVE A CLUE WHAT'S GOING ON WITH THEM.

Panel 4:
AH...THE GIDDINESS OF INSIGHT...

I'M FAIRLY SURE THIS IS AS CLOSE AS WE'RE GOING TO GET.

Panel 5:
I HAVEN'T TALKED TO YOU ALL WEEK, CATHY. WHAT'S NEW?

NOTHING, REALLY, MOM.

Panel 6:
WHAT DID YOU DO ALL WEEK?

NOTHING MUCH.

Panel 7:
DID YOU GO ANYWHERE NEW? DO ANYTHING DIFFERENT??

NOT REALLY.

Panel 8:
NOW THAT I FINALLY HAVE TIME TO RECORD THINGS IN THE BABY BOOK, THERE'S NEVER ANYTHING TO REPORT.

OUR BABY

Panel 9:
THE HEAVY, HUMID AIR IN THE BATHROOM MADE THE SCALE REGISTER TOO HIGH!

Panel 10:
THE HUMID AIR SEEPED INTO THE CLOSET, GOT THE CLOTHES DAMP AND MADE THEM SHRINK WHEN I TURNED ON THE FURNACE!

Panel 11:
THE COMBINED HUMIDITY AND DRYNESS WARPED THE DOOR THE MIRROR IS ATTACHED TO, CAUSING THE MIRROR TO RIPPLE AND GIVE THE ILLUSION THAT MY THIGHS HAVE GROWN!!

Panel 12:
AND WHAT ARE YOU SO HAPPY FOR??

I LOVE THE SOUND OF IMPENDING DOUGHNUTS.

RUSTLE RUSTLE RUSTLE

SNORE Z Z Z Z

BAM! CRASH! CLANK!

SNORE Z Z Z

CRUNCH

YAP YAP YAP

HOW COMFORTING TO KNOW YOU'D WAKE UP IF A BURGLAR EVER STOPPED IN THE KITCHEN FOR A SNACK.

WHAT ELSE DO WE REALLY THINK IS WORTH GUARDING?

COOKIES

...WHAT? NOW WHAT? WHAT DO YOU WANT, ELECTRA?

YOU'VE HAD DINNER, BEEN FOR A WALK... I'VE BRUSHED YOU, PETTED YOU, PLAYED ALL YOUR FAVORITE GAMES...

YOU HAVE TOYS, BONES, TREATS, WATER...QUIT STARING AT ME AND FIND SOMETHING FUN TO DO!!

ELECTRA

IT WOULD BE HARD TO FIND ANYTHING THAT COULD TOP THIS.

THE WARRIORS HAVE RETURNED!

YOU ACTUALLY SURVIVED A FIVE-DAY RETREAT IN THE WOODS??

HAH! ON DAY ONE WE CALLED A CAB ON FRED'S CELLULAR PHONE, BEAT A PATH BACK TO THE HOTEL AND BRIBED A GUY TO HOOK UP THE SPORTS CHANNEL!

YOU ABANDONED THE GROUP AND SAT IN A HOTEL FOR FOUR DAYS??

IT COST $1,200, BUT WE DID IT! WE DISCOVERED THE MALE WITHIN!

HE LIKES TO WATCH SPORTS ON TV AND ORDER ROOM SERVICE.

IT'S TOO LATE TO START ANY BIG PROJECTS FOR THE YEAR, BUT TOO EARLY TO START PANICKING FOR THE HOLIDAYS...

IT'S TOO LATE TO GET ORGANIZED FOR 1991, BUT TOO EARLY TO LAUNCH INTO THE ALL-NEW, 1992 SYSTEM...

IT'S TOO LATE TO LOSE ANY REAL WEIGHT THIS YEAR, BUT TOO EARLY TO START THE NEW YEAR'S DIET...

NOVEMBER 26: KICK-OFF DATE OF THE PRE-HOLIDAY COMA.

AS SOON AS THANKSGIVING GETS CLOSE, I START EATING. I EAT BECAUSE I KNOW I'M GOING TO SEE MY MOTHER.

I WANT TO SHOW MOM THAT MY WEIGHT-LOSS PLAN WORKS BETTER THAN HER WEIGHT-LOSS PLAN. THE PRESSURE MAKES ME NERVOUS, SO I EAT.

THE MORE DETERMINED I AM TO PROVE THAT I HAVE CONQUERED THE FAMILY EATING PROBLEM, THE MORE I EAT.

I'M HOME, MOTHER.

I BELIEVE WE HAVE A TIE THIS YEAR, DEAR.

TIME OUT! NO MORE PIE!

ME EITHER! NO MORE PIE!

WELL, OK...ONE LITTLE SLICE, JUST TO EVEN IT OFF AT THE HALF...

OOPS. YOU WENT OVER. HERE. I'LL TRIM THIS OFF...

...WAIT...I'LL GET THIS SLIVER TO FINISH AN EVEN THREE-QUARTERS...

NO! I HAVE THAT ONE!

NO, I HAVE IT!

NO, I....

WHAT'S ALL THE COMMOTION?

WE'RE TWO MINUTES INTO THE FOURTH QUARTER.

AND WE HAVE ANOTHER FIRST DOWN.

DUE TO THE TIGHT ECONOMY, YOUR FATHER AND I HAVE DECIDED TO ELIMINATE GIFT-GIVING THIS CHRISTMAS, CATHY.

NO GIFTS?

WELL, WE'LL HAVE TO GIVE GIFTS TO SOME OF MY PROBLEM CLIENTS...

AND WE'LL HAVE TO GIVE GIFTS TO ANYONE WE OFFENDED DURING THE YEAR...

AND WE'LL HAVE TO GIVE GIFTS TO THE RELATIVES WE CAN'T DUMP FROM THE LIST BECAUSE THEY KEEP SENDING US GIFTS, BUT THAT'S IT!!

WE'LL BE GIVING GIFTS ONLY TO THOSE PEOPLE WE DON'T LIKE AND AREN'T SPEAKING TO.

ANOTHER HAPPY AMERICAN FAMILY REDISCOVERS THE BASICS.

OH, NO, MOM. HERE'S THE SAME SCARF YOU BOUGHT EARLIER FOR $3.00 LESS.

OH, DEAR. WE'LL HAVE TO RETURN THE FIRST ONE.

THE STORE WE HAVE TO RETURN IT TO IS TWO LEVELS UP, THREE WINGS OVER AND A MILE IN THE OPPOSITE DIRECTION!

BUT IT'S $3.00 LESS HERE. WE HAVE TO RETURN IT!

IT'LL TAKE THE REST OF THE DAY TO GO ALL THAT WAY AND RETURN IT!

BUT IF WE DON'T, WE'LL HAVE THROWN $3.00 AWAY FOR NOTHING!

TWO WOMEN, FROZEN ON LEVEL #3, IN FRONT OF STORE #764, GRAPPLE WITH MORAL DILEMMA #995.

NO IDEA WHERE WE PARKED THE CAR?

NONE.

THANK HEAVENS YOUR FATHER CAN'T SEE THIS, AFTER ALL HIS LECTURES!

WANDERING AROUND LIKE ZOMBIES...HOO, BOY! HE'D GO CRAZY!

HOO, HA!! IF YOUR FATHER WERE HERE, HE'D HAVE A CONNIPTION!

HA, HA! HOO HA!! HE'D GO BERSERK!

...THEN AGAIN, HE'D KNOW WHERE THE CAR WAS...

MAKES YOU KIND OF NUTS, DOESN'T IT?

THERE'S A SALES-PERSON, CATHY.

OH, NO! NOT HER! I MADE HER UNDO A WHOLE DISPLAY AND THEN DIDN'T BUY THE ITEM.

THERE'S ANOTHER ONE.

HER?? NO! I BEGGED HER TO PUT FOUR THINGS ON HOLD AND THEN NEVER CAME BACK!

HOW ABOUT THAT ONE?

AACK! NO! I RETURNED SOMETHING TO HER SIX MONTHS AFTER THE FACT! I CAN'T FACE HER!

MY GIRLFRIEND WANTS TO KNOW IF ALL THE SALESPEOPLE ARE OUT, OR IF YOU HAVE SOME OTHER ONES HIDDEN IN THE BACK ROOM.

THINK OF THE MALL AS AN 18-HOLE GOLF COURSE, IRVING...

YOU ARE **NOT** DRAGGING ME TO THE END OF THIS MALL AGAIN!

IT'S THE SAME COURSE, AND YET A DIFFERENT EXPERIENCE EVERY TIME YOU GO THROUGH IT.

MY FEET HURT!

WE'VE JUST FINISHED NINE HOLES AND ARE TEEING UP FOR THE SUPREME TEST OF MENTAL AND PHYSICAL FINESSE ON HOLE NUMBER...

I'M TIRED BORED SWEATY AND I'M GOING HOME!

ANOTHER SHOPPER DISCOVERS HOW VERY LITTLE HUMOR THERE IS IN THE EXPERIENCE OF TRYING TO HUMOR SOMEONE.

BOUTIQ

FOOD, FAMILY, FRIENDS...

LOVE, HEALTH, HAPPINESS...

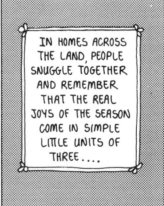

IN HOMES ACROSS THE LAND, PEOPLE SNUGGLE TOGETHER AND REMEMBER THAT THE REAL JOYS OF THE SEASON COME IN SIMPLE LITTLE UNITS OF THREE....

A WOMAN, A PHONE, AN INFOMERCIAL.

WHAT DO YOU MEAN, ALL THE OPERATORS ARE BUSY??!!

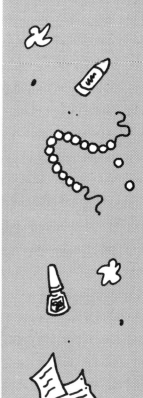

THE SIMPLE GIFT OF HOMEMADE COOKIES MEANS MORE THAN ANYTHING MONEY CAN BUY, CATHY!

WE'VE MADE TWO BATCHES OF DOUGH TO PRODUCE SIX COOKIES, MOM.

...OOPS! THIS ONE'S A LITTLE BROWN AROUND THE EDGES!

TWO BATCHES OF DOUGH TO PRODUCE **FIVE** COOKIES.

...OOPS! SANTA'S LITTLE HEAD SNAPPED OFF!

FOUR COOKIES...

...THIS TREE IS CROOKED!

THREE COOKIES...

...OOPS!

I FEEL ILL.

...BUT ILL IN A HAPPY HOLIDAYS KIND OF WAY.

ATTENTION ALL EMPLOYEES: GIFT CATALOG SHIPMENTS HAVE ARRIVED FOR CATHY, RICHARD, BARBARA, GERRY AND...

LET ME SEE! LET ME SEE!

WHAT DID YOU ORDER?

WHO'S IT FOR?

LET ME TRY IT ON!

WHERE'D YOU GET IT?

LET ME SEE!

IS THIS AN OFFICE OR A SHOPPING MALL??

MALL!

THE ANNUAL HOLIDAY MUTINY HAS BEGUN.

ARE YOU KIDDING?? IT STARTED ON NOVEMBER 4 THIS YEAR.

FIRST I HAVE TO READ ALL THE CARDS IN THE STORE...THEN I'LL PICK A NICE GENERAL ONE THAT MATCHES MY PERSONALITY AND ARTISTIC TASTE AND WILL BE MY OVERALL HOLIDAY STATEMENT FOR THE YEAR...

THEN I HAVE TO PICK OUT SOME SPECIAL FUNNY ONES FOR SOME OF MY FRIENDS...THEN I HAVE TO TRY TO REMEMBER WHICH FUNNY ONES I SENT TO WHICH FRIENDS LAST YEAR SO I WON'T SEND THE SAME ONES THIS YEAR...

THEN I HAVE TO FIND SOME BACK-UP FUNNY ONES... THEN I HAVE TO GO BACK AND READ ALL THE CARDS AGAIN TO MAKE SURE I GOT THE PERFECT ONES... THEN I'LL....

THE CARD STORE: WOMEN'S REVENGE FOR MONDAY NIGHT FOOTBALL.

TO JAN, WHO SENT A CARD STAMPED WITH HER NAME, I SEND A PERSONALLY SIGNED CARD AND A THOUGHTFUL NOTE.

TO RUTH, WHO SENT A ONE-PAGE, PRE-PRINTED LETTER, I SEND A THREE-PAGE, HANDWRITTEN LETTER AND SIX PHOTOS!

TO SHEILA, WHO SENT A CARD, A LETTER AND PHOTOS, I SEND A VIDEO, A POEM AND A PRESSED WILDFLOWER I'VE SAVED FOR HER SINCE OUR FIFTH-GRADE GIRL SCOUT CAMP-OUT! HAH! TOP **THAT**, SHEILA!!

I'VE MOVED BEYOND HOLIDAY GREETINGS AND AM INTO HOLIDAY GUILTINGS.

WHY AM I NERVOUS ABOUT GOING TO MY PARENTS' HOUSE FOR CHRISTMAS?? THEY LIVE IN TOWN. I SEE THEM ALL THE TIME.

I'M JUST SPENDING A FEW DAYS UNDER THEIR ROOF. WHAT COULD HAPPEN? SLEEPING IN THE LITTLE BED I GREW UP IN. WHAT'S THE BIG DEAL??

WHAT COULD THEY SAY? WHAT COULD THEY DO? WHAT COULD POSSIBLY MAKE ME CRAZY THIS YEAR??

PREPARING FOR ANY CON-TINGENCY, ANOTHER WOMAN PACKS HER INNER SUITCASE.

READY FOR A NICE BIG BREAK-FAST, CATHY?

NO TIME FOR BREAKFAST, MOM! I HAVE TO FINISH MY CHRISTMAS CARDS...

...FINISH MY SHOPPING... WRAP ALL MY GIFTS...MAIL THE PACKAGES...DO MY LAUNDRY...HEM AND IRON MY HOLIDAY OUTFIT...GET MY HAIR TRIMMED AND DO ALL THE WORK I DIDN'T DO LAST WEEK AT THE OFFICE!!

GMBK

...IS THERE MORE MILK?

YOU CAN COME OUT NOW, DAD. THE TRANQUILIZATION PROCESS IS COMPLETE.

NO ONE HAS ANY CONFIDENCE IN THE ECONOMY THIS HOLIDAY SEASON, MOM. IT'S ALL THEY'VE TALKED ABOUT THIS YEAR.

NO ONE HAS ANY MONEY... NO ONE HAS ANY JOB SECURITY... NO ONE HAS ANY HOPE THAT IT'S GOING TO GET ANY BETTER.

LEVEL SEVEN

HOW COMFORTING TO SEE THAT EVERYONE STILL SEEMS TO HAVE A CAR.

LOT FULL

MERRY CHRISTMAS, DEAR FAMILY! BEFORE WE BEGIN, I JUST WANT TO SAY...

Whirrr...

WAIT! DON'T TAKE MY PICTURE! I NEED SOME MAKEUP!

I HAVE TO BRUSH MY HAIR!

I HAVE TO GET OUT OF THIS OLD BATHROBE!

I LOOK TOO FAT IN THIS SWEATSUIT!

GIVE ME A MINUTE!

GIVE ME TEN MINUTES!

GIVE US HALF AN HOUR!

ONE HOUR, TOPS!

...THE LENGTH OF THE FESTIVITIES IS DIRECTLY PROPORTIONAL TO THE NUMBER OF WOMEN IN THE HOUSEHOLD.

DO YOU WANT TO GO TO THE MOVIES WITH IRVING AND ME TONIGHT?

US?? YES! YOU WANT YOUR PARENTS TO COME?? YES!

WE WERE THINKING OF "BUGSY", "JFK", "PRINCE OF TIDES" OR...

YES!! WE'LL GO! WE WANT TO GO!! YES!!

DON'T YOU EVEN CARE WHAT YOU SEE??

WE'RE GOING TO THE MOVIES WITH CATHY!! WE'RE GOING TO THE MOVIES WITH CATHY!!

THERE'S ONLY ONE PLOT THAT REALLY SUSTAINS YOUR MOTHER'S INTEREST.

MY DAUGHTER WANTS ME WITH HER!!

Panel 1: DON'T FILL UP ON POPCORN! WE HAVE ALL THAT NICE FOOD AT HOME! / GET MY MOTHER A POPCORN, IRVING.

Panel 2: SHE SAID SHE DOESN'T WANT POPCORN. / OH, NO! NO POPCORN! / SHE WANTS POPCORN.

Panel 3: ON THIS PARTICULAR SUBJECT, YOU'RE SUPPOSED TO IGNORE ALL THE VERBS AND ADVERBS AND DO WHATEVER THE NOUN IS.

Panel 4: TO GET ALONG WITH OUR FAMILY, YOU HAVE TO UNDERSTAND THE LANGUAGE OF FOOD. / NO BUTTER! DID I MENTION NO BUTTER?!

Panel 5: AS YOUR MOTHER, I KNOW YOU HAVE TO GO HOME... BUT AS YOUR MOTHER, I WANT YOU TO STAY HERE FOREVER, CATHY.

Panel 6: AS YOUR MOTHER, I KNOW YOU HAVE YOUR OWN LIFE TO LIVE... ...BUT AS YOUR MOTHER, I WANT TO GET TO WATCH EVERY MINUTE OF IT.

Panel 7: AS YOUR MOTHER, I'M BURSTING WITH PRIDE FOR ALL YOU'VE DONE... BUT AS YOUR MOTHER, I SEE NO REASON FOR YOU TO DO ANYTHING BUT SIT RIGHT HERE ON MY LAP.

Panel 8: IT'S HARD TO SEPARATE MY CAREER FROM THE REST OF MY LIFE WHEN THEY'RE BOTH THE SAME THING.

Panel 9: I THOUGHT WE'D GO SOMEWHERE REALLY ELEGANT THIS NEW YEAR'S EVE, CATHY. / BLACK TIE. LONG DRESS. OK. I HAVE THAT.

Panel 10: THEN I THOUGHT IT WOULD BE MORE FUN TO GO TO A PARTY. / DRESSY SHORT DRESS. I HAVE THAT... MEDIUM DRESSY DRESS. I HAVE THAT.

Panel 11: THEN I THOUGHT WE SHOULD JUST HAVE A SPECIAL NIGHT AT HOME. WHAT DO YOU SAY?

Panel 12: AACK! "FESTIVE CASUAL"!! THE NIGHTMARE CATEGORY!!

SOMEONE DRANK MY ULTRA SLIM-FAST SHAKE!

SOMEONE ATE MY JENNY CRAIG LUNCH!

SOMEONE TOOK MY NUTRI-SYSTEM SNACK!!

SOMEONE ATE MY WEIGHT WATCHERS BREAD EXCHANGE!

WELCOME TO THE OFFICE OF 1992, MR. PINKLEY.

WE'RE CHEATING ON OUR DIETS WITH OTHER PEOPLE'S DIET FOOD.

SOMEONE'S BEEN INTO MY METAMUCIL COOKIES!!

"SINCE TODAY IS THE FIRST MONDAY OF THE YEAR, NEW YEAR'S DIETS DON'T TECHNICALLY COUNT UNTIL TODAY."

WHAT?? WE STARTED OUR DIETS LAST WEDNESDAY!

I GUESS WE'RE FIVE DAYS AHEAD OF EVERYONE.

WE'VE BEEN DIETING FOR FIVE DAYS AND EVERYONE ELSE HAS BEEN HAVING A FREE-FOR-ALL??

WE HAD FIVE DAYS OF ANGUISH FOR NOTHING?? HAH!! WE GET A BONUS FIVE DAYS THIS YEAR!! A BONUS FIVE DAYS OF CHEATING FOR CATHY AND CHARLENE!!

THERE'S NOTHING LIKE A DIET BUDDY TO INSPIRE THAT WINNING ATTITUDE...

THE KEY TO WEIGHT LOSS IS LEARNING TO THINK OF IT AS LITTLE UNITS OF WEIGHT TO LOSE, NOT ONE IMPOSSIBLE CHUNK!

THINK OF IT AS LITTLE MANAGEABLE UNITS... LITTLE TINY UNITS... TINY BITE-SIZED UNITS..

...LITTLE TEENY, TINY, BITE-SIZED, CANDY-COATED CHOCOLATE UNITS...

IT'S GETTING IMPOSSIBLE TO COME UP WITH A DIET PHILOSOPHY THAT DOESN'T HURL ME RIGHT BACK TO THE M&M STASH.

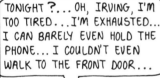
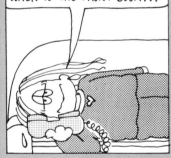

47

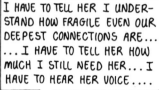

OUT! OUT! OUT! OUT! OUT! OUT!

...BUT MAYBE I'LL WANT THIS LATER... MAYBE I'LL CHANGE MY MIND... MAYBE I NEED THIS MORE THAN I KNOW...

IT'S BEEN PART OF MY LIFE FOR SO LONG... IF I JUST TOSS IT ASIDE NOW I COULD SPEND THE REST OF MY DAYS TRYING TO GET IT BACK!

THE SKILLS I'VE PERFECTED IN SABOTAGING MY PERSONAL LIFE ARE NOW BEING APPLIED TO MY DESK.

PHIL'S LETTER ARRIVED AND I FAXED MY REPLY! IT'S BACK IN HIS LAP!

HERE, HE ALREADY FAXED BACK TO YOUR FAX.

WHAT?? IT'S BACK IN MY LAP? HAH!! I'LL FAX BACK TO HIS FAX!

...HE FAXED BACK AGAIN.
THEN I'LL FAX BACK!
...HE FAXED BACK AGAIN.
THEN I'LL FAX BACK!!

PHIL LEFT A MESSAGE ON YOUR VOICE MAIL WHILE YOU WERE FAXING YOUR LAST FAX.

EFFICIENCY WIPES OUT ANOTHER MORNING.

ATTENTION ALL EMPLOYEES: A SURVEILLANCE CAMERA HAS BEEN INSTALLED IN THE COFFEE ROOM.

THE NEXT PERSON WHO LEAVES AN EMPTY POT ON THE COFFEE MAKER, DIRTY DISHES IN THE SINK OR OLD PIZZA IN THE REFRIGERATOR WILL BE VIDEOTAPED AND HELD UP FOR PUBLIC RIDICULE AT OUR NEXT MEETING!!

WHAT DO YOU HAVE TO SAY ABOUT **THAT**?!

I HAVE TO GO FIX MY MAKEUP.

I HAVE TO PUT SOME MOUSSE IN MY HAIR.

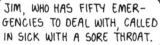

I KNOW YOU'RE WORRIED BECAUSE I'M TOO SICK TO GO TO WORK TODAY, ELECTRA...

YAP YAP YAP

YOU KNOW SOMETHING'S WRONG AND YOU DON'T KNOW HOW TO FIX IT...

YAP YAP YAP

YOU'RE TRYING TO SAY YOU'D DO ANYTHING FOR ME... OH, ELECTRA...

YAP YAP YAP YAP YAP

MOMMY WOULD WEEP WITH EMOTION, BUT THE TEARS WOULD FREEZE ON HER FACE.

CATHY'S SICK.

OF COURSE SHE IS. DID SHE GET THE FLU SHOT LIKE I TOLD HER TO?...NO.

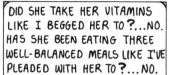

DID SHE TAKE HER VITAMINS LIKE I BEGGED HER TO?...NO. HAS SHE BEEN EATING THREE WELL-BALANCED MEALS LIKE I'VE PLEADED WITH HER TO?...NO.

OH, MY POOR BABY! YOU'RE SICK! LET ME HELP YOU! LET ME TAKE CARE OF YOU! I'M ON MY WAY, MY POOR BABY!

MY NEED TO FEED HER SOUP SURPASSED MY NEED TO GLOAT.

IT WAS SO NICE OF YOU TO BRING "GET WELL" FLOWERS TO CATHY, IRVING!

MY MOTHER AND MY BOYFRIEND ARE IN THE KITCHEN TOGETHER.

CATHY'S FATHER USED TO BRING ME FLOWERS BEFORE WE WERE **MARRIED**... OF COURSE, HE BROUGHT ME FLOWERS **AFTER** WE WERE MARRIED, TOO! NOT THAT WE'RE EVEN **TALKING** ABOUT **MARRIAGE**....

...HOO, HA!...THEN AGAIN, NOTHING CAN LIFT A WOMAN'S SPIRITS LIKE FLOWERS... ...UNLESS, OF COURSE, IT **IS** A **PROPOSAL** OF....

MOTHER.

WHY, LOOK! SHE'S OUT OF BED ALREADY!

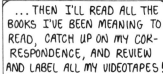

HOW ARE THINGS GOING WITH IRVING, CATHY?

OH, THEY'RE PERFECT! JUST PERFECT!

...WELL, MAYBE NOT PERFECT, BUT THEY'RE GREAT... WELL, THEY'RE PRETTY GOOD... THEY'RE GOOD... THEY'RE NICE... THEY'RE OK... THEY'RE AVERAGE....

...THEY'RE... HELP! I CAN'T STOP MYSELF!...THEY'RE FAIR...THEY'RE MEDIOCRE...THEY'RE STOP ME, CHARLENE... THEY'RE HOPELESS... THEY'RE PATHETIC...THEY'RE ....

WELCOME TO THE PRE-VALENTINE'S DAY FREE-FALL OF EMOTIONAL CONFIDENCE.

THEY'RE DOOMED...

"IT'S ALMOST VALENTINE'S DAY. DO YOU KNOW WHERE YOUR RELATIONSHIP IS GOING?"

WHY DOES IT ALWAYS HAVE TO BE GOING SOMEWHERE?

WHEN PEOPLE ARE MARRIED, NO ONE ASKS IF THEIR RELATIONSHIP IS GOING ANYWHERE.

WHY IS IT GREAT FOR MARRIED PEOPLE TO BE CONTENT...BUT WHEN SINGLE PEOPLE ARE CONTENT EVERYONE SAYS WE'RE TRAPPED IN A PARANOID RUT THAT WILL SAP THE LIFE OUT OF THE RELATIONSHIP IF IT DOESN'T "GO SOMEWHERE"?!!

I THINK SIMON'S GOING TO PROPOSE.

AACK!

A MAGAZINE CAN LEAD US TO THE EDGE, BUT IT STILL TAKES A GIRLFRIEND TO SHOVE US OVER THE BRINK.

HAVE YOU EVER CALLED A MAN WHEN YOU WERE IN THIS STATE OF MIND AND NOT REGRETTED IT?

NO.

HAVE YOU EVER FELT THIS WAY AND NOT TOTALLY HUMILIATED YOURSELF?

NO.

HAS ANYTHING IN YOUR LIFE MADE YOU FEEL THAT CALLING HIM NOW WOULD BE ANYTHING LESS THAN A DISASTER?

NO.

THEN, BY ALL MEANS, GIVE HIM A CALL!

I LOVE A FRIEND WHO'S WILLING TO LOOK PAST THE OBVIOUS.

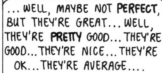

I'LL GET IRVING A ROMANTIC VALENTINE AND MAKE HIM SQUIRM UNDER THE PRESSURE... NO. I'LL GET HIM AN ALOOF VALENTINE AND MAKE HIM WONDER IF I CARE...

NO. I'LL GET HIM A VALENTINE SO OBSCURE THAT NO MATTER HOW HE INTERPRETS IT, HE'LL BE CONVINCED I MEANT SOMETHING ELSE!

...NO! I'LL GET HIM AN ASSORTMENT! A BOMBARDMENT OF CONFUSION! HA, HA!! HE WON'T HAVE A CLUE WHAT'S GOING ON!!

FOR THE ONE I LOVE: SEASON TICKETS TO THE LOONEY BOWL.

SNAP SNAP STUFF STUFF

WAD RIP RIP STUFF HOOK RIP

SNAP STUFF RIP STOMP STOMP STOMP!

HOW MUCH MORE LINGERIE MUST I BUY BEFORE I OWN MY WOMANHOOD?

CHOCOLATE IN THE GROCERY STORE... CHOCOLATE IN THE DRUGSTORE... CHOCOLATE AT THE CAR WASH... CHOCOLATE EVERYWHERE...

CHOCOLATE FUMES FILLING THE AIR...SEEPING INTO MY BRAIN. DISTORTING MY PERSPECTIVE... OBLITERATING MY FOCUS... I CAN'T THINK...CAN'T WORK ...CAN'T TALK... CAN'T...

I WASN'T TRYING TO EAT IT SO MUCH AS I WAS TRYING TO DESTROY IT.

WHAT WERE WE THINKING, TRYING ON THIS RIDICULOUS LINGERIE??

WHO KNOWS? I JUST WANTED TO SEE WHAT ALL THE FUSS WAS ABOUT.

I GUESS EVERYONE HAS TO TRY IT AT LEAST ONCE.

HA, HA! ONCE IS ENOUGH!

DOES ANYONE EVER BUY THIS STUFF??

WHO KNOWS?! HA, HA!!

CATHY! HOW'D THAT LITTLE NEW YEAR'S PEEK-A-BOO TEDDY WORK OUT FOR YOU??

THE ONLY TIME A SALESCLERK HAS EVER ACKNOWLEDGED MY EXISTENCE IS TO SHAME ME.

...AND CHARLENE! I THINK YOUR SPECIAL ORDER IS IN!!

SIMON'S BEEN SO STRANGE LATELY... I CAN FEEL THE TENSION... IT'S ALL OVER HIS FACE ... IT'S IN EVERY GESTURE... THERE'S SOMETHING HE WANTS TO SAY... HE'S SEARCHING FOR THE WORDS....

OH, CATHY, HE'S GOING TO PROPOSE ON VALENTINE'S DAY!!

EITHER THAT OR HE'S PLANNING TO BREAK UP.

THE GREAT ONES WALK THE FINE LINE RIGHT UNTIL THE END...

I SENT SIMON A GIANT BOUQUET OF FLOWERS FOR VALENTINE'S DAY.

REALLY?? YOU SENT FLOWERS TO A MAN??

MEN LOVE GETTING FLOWERS FROM WOMEN!

A GIFT OF FLOWERS TELLS MEN WE'RE NOT ONLY IN TOUCH WITH OUR FEELINGS, BUT CONFIDENT ENOUGH TO EXPRESS THEM IN A BEAUTIFUL AND GRACIOUS MANNER!!

ALSO, I ENCLOSED A GIFT CARD MENTIONING THAT IF HE DOESN'T COME UP WITH AN ENGAGEMENT RING TONIGHT, I WALK.

AH... THE OLD-FASHIONED TOUCH.

61

IT'S NORMAL TO HAVE CONFLICTING FEELINGS WHEN A GIRL-FRIEND GETS MARRIED, CATHY.

NOT ME. I'M FINE.

IT REALLY HELPS TO TALK IT THROUGH.

I'M THRILLED FOR HER.

WE'RE HERE FOR YOU, 24 HOURS A DAY. ANY TIME YOU WANT TO TALK, JUST CALL.

NOTHING TO TALK ABOUT. I'M PERFECTLY FINE.

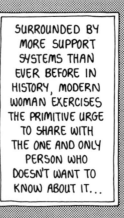

SURROUNDED BY MORE SUPPORT SYSTEMS THAN EVER BEFORE IN HISTORY, MODERN WOMAN EXERCISES THE PRIMITIVE URGE TO SHARE WITH THE ONE AND ONLY PERSON WHO DOESN'T WANT TO KNOW ABOUT IT...

CHARLENE AND SIMON ARE GETTING MARRIED, IRVING!!

AACK! I'M NOT LISTENING! NOT LISTENING!!

WHAT DID THE PEOPLE AT WORK SAY WHEN YOU TOLD THEM ABOUT OUR WEDDING, SIMON?

I DIDN'T TELL THEM, CHARLENE.

WHAT DID YOUR FRIENDS SAY?

I DIDN'T TELL THEM.

WHO DID YOU TELL?

I DIDN'T TELL ANYONE.

WHO DID YOU HINT TO?

I DIDN'T HINT.

WE'VE BEEN ENGAGED FOR TEN DAYS AND YOU HAVEN'T BREATHED A PEEP OF IT TO ANYONE???

NO.

IT'S A WONDER MEN DON'T JUST EXPLODE.

I THOUGHT YOU DIDN'T LIKE GOING TO MOVIES AT THE MALL, SIMON.

I WANT TO DO SOME SHOPPING BEFORE THE SHOW.

SHOPPING?? SHOPPING FOR WHAT?? HEE, HEE! AS IF I DIDN'T KNOW!

I NEED A COUPLE OF SHIRTS.

SHIRTS! HA, HA! YOU'RE SUCH A KIDDER! YOU'RE SO CUTE! HOO, HA, HA! SHIRTS!!

THE MEN'S STORE IS THIS WAY, HONEY!

GET OUT THE WINDEX! THERE'S ANOTHER POTENTIAL BRIDE STUCK TO THE WINDOW!

WHEN SIMON SAID HE LIKED ME, I PUSHED HIM TO SAY HE LOVED ME... HE SAID HE LOVED ME, AND I PUSHED HIM TO MARRY ME...

HE FINALLY SAID HE WANTS TO MARRY ME, AND I'M PUSHING HIM TO PLAN EVERY DETAIL OF THE WEDDING!

EACH TIME HE DOES WHAT I WANT, I PUSH HIM TO THE NEXT LEVEL OF DISCOMFORT! WHY CAN'T I JUST RELAX AND ENJOY THE MOMENT WE'RE IN?!

RING RING

OK, CHARLENE. I'LL TALK ABOUT THE WEDDING TONIGHT IF YOU WANT.

WHEN DO YOU THINK YOU'LL WANT TO START OUR FAMILY??!

SIMON AND CHARLENE ARE GETTING MARRIED, MOM.

SIMON?? YOUR SIMON??

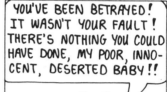

WE ONLY DATED A FEW TIMES. HE'S NOT MY SIMON.

YOU PRIMED HIM FOR MARRIAGE, AND THEN YOUR BEST FRIEND SNATCHED HIM AWAY!!

YOU'VE BEEN BETRAYED! IT WASN'T YOUR FAULT! THERE'S NOTHING YOU COULD HAVE DONE, MY POOR, INNOCENT, DESERTED BABY!!

...CATHY BLEW IT WITH ANOTHER ONE.

I'M NOT UPSET THAT CHARLENE'S GETTING MARRIED, MOM!

ON THE SURFACE, YOU'RE NOT UPSET, BUT DEEP DOWN, YOU'RE UPSET.

I'M NOT UPSET!

ON THE FIRST LEVEL DOWN, YOU'RE NOT UPSET... ON THE SECOND LEVEL DOWN, YOU'RE NOT UPSET... BUT IF YOU DIG **DEEP, DEEP** DOWN, ON SOME LEVEL YOU'RE....

AAUGH!

BINGO! LEVEL SIX! YOU'RE UPSET!

WHAT A MOTHER DOESN'T KNOW FOR SURE SHE CAN MAKE HAPPEN ANYWAY.

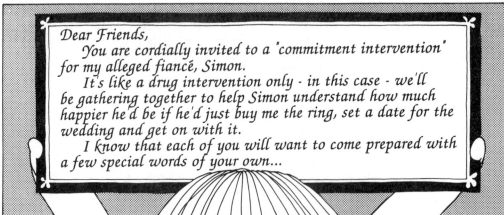

Dear Friends,
    You are cordially invited to a "commitment intervention" for my alleged fiancé, Simon.
    It's like a drug intervention only - in this case - we'll be gathering together to help Simon understand how much happier he'd be if he'd just buy me the ring, set a date for the wedding and get on with it.
    I know that each of you will want to come prepared with a few special words of your own...

ARE YOU OUT OF YOUR MIND, CHARLENE?!

GOOD! THAT'S THE SPIRIT! ONLY MORE PASSION, AND, OF COURSE, YOU'LL BE SAYING IT TO **SIMON**, NOT ME!

HI! IS THIS SIMON'S MOTHER?

YES. WHO'S CALLING?

IT'S CHARLENE! I CAN'T BELIEVE I'VE DATED SIMON FOR THREE YEARS AND HAVEN'T MET YOU YET! I FEEL I ALREADY KNOW YOU SO WELL!

ANYWAY, SINCE SIMON'S HAVING SO MUCH TROUBLE DEALING WITH OUR WEDDING, I'M INVITING SOME FRIENDS AND FAMILY OVER TO HELP HIM WORK THROUGH HIS COMMITMENT PROBLEM.

WHO IS THIS??

CHARLENE! HIS **SWEETHEART**, CHARLENE!

...HONEY, DID SIMON EVER MENTION GOING OUT WITH SOMEONE NAMED CHARLENE??

WHO??

CHARLENE WANTS US TO COME TO A LITTLE GATHERING TO HELP SIMON FACE HIS COMMITMENT PROBLEM.

WHAT PROBLEM? HE SAID HE WANTS TO MARRY HER.

WELL, YES. BUT NOW HE WON'T DISCUSS IT.

HE SAID HE'D DO IT. WHY DOES HE HAVE TO DISCUSS IT?

BECAUSE SAYING HE'D DO IT DOESN'T COUNT IF HE WON'T DISCUSS PLANS TO MAKE IT HAPPEN!!

IF HE GOT THE WORD "MARRIAGE" OUT OF HIS MOUTH ONE TIME, HE IS RELEASED FROM ALL CONVERSATION ON THE SUBJECT FOR THE NEXT YEAR!

WILL YOU AND IRVING BE COMING, OR SHALL I ADD YOU TO THE LIST OF COUPLES WHO BROKE UP DISCUSSING THE INVITATION?

I CAN BE FAT AND PRODUCTIVE OR THIN AND COMATOSE... IS THIS WHAT IT'S COME TO??

AS LONG AS I EAT WHAT I WANT I'M FULLY FUNCTIONAL... ...BUT AS SOON AS I USE SOME SELF-CONTROL, I'M INCAPABLE OF THINKING ONE COHERENT THOUGHT??!

DOES IT HAVE TO USE 100% OF MY BRAIN CELLS TO FOCUS ON NOT EATING SOMETHING I SHOULDN'T BE EATING??!

I WOULDN'T GO IN THERE YET. CATHY'S STILL IN CONFERENCE WITH MR. MUFFIN.

IT TOOK TWO MUFFINS TO GET THROUGH THE FILMORE CRISIS THIS MORNING...

...HALF A PIZZA TO DEAL WITH THE BEEKMAN DISASTER... A PASTA SALAD TO NEUTRALIZE THE PIZZA...

...AND A BAG OF MICROWAVE POPCORN TO RALLY FROM MY FAT DEPRESSION LONG ENOUGH TO ANSWER SOME PHONE CALLS.

DID YOU DRINK YOUR EIGHT GLASSES OF WATER?

NO. I DIDN'T WANT TO FEEL BLOATED.

YOU WANT TO PLAY? OK! GET THE BALL, ELECTRA!

GOOD GIRL! GET THE BALL, ELECTRA! GOOD GIRL! GET THE BALL, ELECTRA!

WHEW! I'M EXHAUSTED! LET'S LIE DOWN AND WATCH TV FOR A FEW HOURS.

MY MASTER, THE WIMP.

THE SHIRTDRESS IS ONE OF THIS SPRING'S FASHION MUSTS.

NICE, SIMPLE LINES... GOOD, HONEST STYLING...

AS WE CELEBRATE A RETURN TO BASICS, THE SHIRTDRESS PERSONIFIES THE CLASSIC FEMALE FORM!

THE EGGPLANT.

NO, THANKS. I'M JUST LOOKING TODAY.

JUST LOOKING??

LOOKING FOR WHAT?? MIGHT THERE BE A BLOUSE IN THE STORE THAT YOU HAVEN'T ALREADY WRINKLED?? MAY I SHOW YOU THE TWO PAIRS OF PANTS YOU HAVEN'T RIPPED OFF THE HANGERS AND LEFT WADDED ON THE FLOOR??

OR WOULD YOU LIKE A CHAIR SO YOU CAN SIT AND LOOK AT **ME** WHILE I TRY TO REASSEMBLE THE 200-UNIT TANK-TOP DISPLAY YOU DESTROYED WHILE BROWSING FOR THE PROPER SIZE OF "MEDIUM"?!!

IS THERE ANY PERRIER?

WHILE THE STORE REMAINS IN BUSINESS, ANOTHER SALESCLERK GOES BELLY-UP.

I WASN'T GOING TO SPEND ANY MONEY, BUT I JUST HAVE TO BUY ONE NEW THING.

IF I BUY ONE NEW THING, I'LL FEEL NEW. IF I FEEL NEW, I'LL ACT NEW...

IF I ACT NEW, I'LL LOSE WEIGHT, EXCEL IN MY JOB, ORGANIZE MY HOME, CATCH UP ON ALL MY CORRESPONDENCE, AND HAVE HORDES OF HANDSOME MEN SHOWERING ME WITH BOUQUETS OF CASABLANCA LILIES!!

...A LOT TO ASK OF A HEADBAND.

HOWEVER, WELL WORTH THE $6.95 TRY.

FOR SPRING: THE SLOUCHY SUIT WITH MIDRIFF-REVEALING BRA TOP IN LAVENDER.	THE CLASSIC CLINGY FLORAL SHIFT IN MAGENTA.	THE SPLIT SKIRT OVER SAUCY HOT PANTS IN CHARTREUSE.	THE SWEATSUIT IN THE DIET FROZEN FOOD SECTION.

THERE ARE THREE WORDS TO DESCRIBE SPRING DRESSING: CLASSIC, CLASSIC AND CLASSIC!	CLASSIC SHAPES, CLASSIC STYLES, ALL DESIGNED TO LAST A LIFETIME!	EACH CLASSIC PIECE IS AN INVESTMENT IN A TIMELESS, ETERNAL LOOK THAT WILL NEVER GO OUT OF STYLE!	...WHEW! HOW LONG UNTIL THIS ONE BLOWS OVER?

WOMAN BUYING A WHITE SHIRT:

BAGGY? REALLY BAGGY? SORT OF BAGGY? OR FITTED? SHEER, SEMI-SHEER OR NON-SHEER? HIGH STAND-UP COLLAR, LOW STAND-UP COLLAR, BUTTON-DOWN COLLAR, TUXEDO COLLAR, NO COLLAR, SCOOP-NECK, BOAT NECK, BOW NECK, V-NECK, OR PLUNGING NECK? TIE BOTTOM, STRAIGHT BOTTOM OR CURVED BOTTOM? COTTON? RAYON? SILK? WASHED SILK? LINEN? LIGHT LINEN? HEAVY LINEN? MEDIUM LINEN? WRINKLY LINEN? LINEN/RAYON BLEND? RAYON/SILK BLEND? RAYON/LINEN/COTTON/SILK BLEND? NORMAL SLEEVE? RAGLAN SLEEVE?

MAN BUYING A WHITE SHIRT:

HERE.

DARING COMBINATIONS OF OLD AND NEW... FANCY AND CASUAL... FORMAL AND FUNKY...

...MORE THAN EVER BEFORE, FASHION IS ABOUT ATTITUDE!

THE FLIRTY ATTITUDE! THE KICKY ATTITUDE! THE SEXY ATTITUDE! AND THIS SEASON'S BIGGY....

I CAN CREATE THOSE LOOKS OUT OF THE JUNK IN MY OWN CLOSET.

...THE BAD ATTITUDE.

OF COURSE, THE DAYS OF WEARING ONE LIP COLOR ARE OUT!

OUT?

OUT. THIS YEAR YOU NEED THE MAUVEY LIP LINER FOLLOWED BY THE TERRA COTTA MATTE CREME, FOLLOWED BY THE SANDSTONE TONE ON TOP!

THREE DIFFERENT HUES TO CREATE A MULTI-DIMENSIONAL SENSUOUS LIP CONTOUR THAT WILL SEND WILD THOUGHTS RACING THROUGH THAT SPECIAL MAN'S MIND....

ONE KISS AND I'LL WIND UP WITH A $15 DRY-CLEANING BILL.

CHARLENE: BAD HAIR DAY.

MARLA: BAD COMPLEXION DAY.

CATHY: BAD HAIR, BAD COMPLEXION AND BAD BODY DAY.

FUNNY HOW PEOPLE ARE ALWAYS DRAWN TO THE OVERACHIEVER.

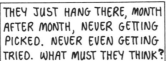

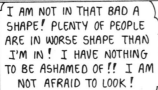

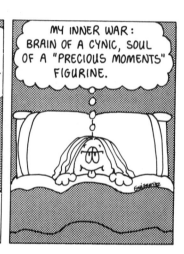

WHAT DID YOU AND IRVING TALK ABOUT THIS WEEK, SWEETIE?

MOM??

WERE THERE ANY SIGNIFICANT CONVERSATIONS?? ANY PARTICULARILY ENDEARING WORDS OR PHRASES??

HUH??

WAS THERE ONE SHRED OF ANYTHING THAT WE COULD INTERPRET AS A SIGN -- HOWEVER BLEAK -- OF RELATIONSHIP MOMENTUM??

MOM...

PRYING IS FOR AMATEURS. I'M INTO SHOVELING.

THE TERM "WHITE-COLLAR WORKER" ORIGINATED IN A 1940 MOVIE WHERE GINGER ROGERS PLAYED A SECRETARY WHO WORE A LITTLE WHITE COLLAR.

HAPPY SECRETARIES' WEEK

IT STARTED A FAD AND FEMALE SECRETARIES OF THE DAY BECAME KNOWN AS "WHITE-COLLAR GIRLS".

HAPPY SECRETARIES' WEEK

HOW IRONIC THAT, 52 YEARS LATER, MEN HAVE CLAIMED THE TITLE "WHITE-COLLAR WORKER" AS A SIGN OF PRESTIGE AND HIGH INCOME... WHILE SECRETARIES -- THE ORIGINAL WHITE-COLLAR WORKERS -- ARE STILL PLEADING FOR RESPECT AND DECENT PAY!

WHAT'S SHE TALKING ABOUT?

CLOTHES. TYPICAL WOMAN.

I GIVE UP.

HAPPY SECRETARIES' WE

WHERE'S MY PEXTON FILE?

RIGHT CORNER OF YOUR DESK.

WHERE'S MY BOSLY CHART?

SECOND DRAWER ON THE LEFT.

HAPPY

WHERE'S MY ATM NUMBER?

BOTTOM OF YOUR PENCIL TRAY.

WHERE'S MY WEISS UPDATE?

TOP BASKET. TWO INCHES DOWN.

WHERE'S MY RAISE?

OOPS! GOTTA GO!

HAPPY SECRETARIES' WEEK

HOW MANY MEGABYTES OF MEMORY MUST I HAVE TO BE COMPATIBLE WITH A TWO-BIT BOSS?

HAPPY SECRETARIES' WEEK

Panel 1: IN HONOR OF EARTH DAY, I TYPED THIS YEAR'S SECRETARIES' DAY MEMO ON RECYCLED PAPER WITH NON-TOXIC INK.

Panel 2: I COPIED IT ON AN ENERGY-EFFICIENT COPIER UNDER LOW-WATTAGE HALOGEN BULBS WHILE DRINKING COFFEE FROM A POLITICALLY CORRECT COUNTRY, IN A REUSABLE CERAMIC MUG, WHICH WAS MADE IN THE U.S.A. BY A NON-POLLUTING COMPANY AND SOLD WITH NO EXCESS PACKAGING!

Panel 3: JUST AS WE'RE LEARNING TO RESPECT THE EARTH, LET US LEARN TO RESPECT THE 18.4 MILLION UNDERPAID SECRETARIES, WITHOUT WHOM THE COMPANIES OF THIS EARTH WOULD SHRIVEL UP AND DIE IN A MATTER OF SECONDS!!

Panel 4: YOU'RE DRIVING ME CRAZY, CHARLENE. AND BURNING NO FOSSIL FUEL IN THE PROCESS!

HAPPY EARTH DAY, HAPPY SECRETARIES' DAY

Panel 5: I TYPE HUNDREDS OF LETTERS FOR $8 AN HOUR ON A $6,000 COMPUTER THAT A $150-AN-HOUR SERVICEMAN COMES TO SERVICE.

Panel 6: I COPY THOUSANDS OF PAGES FOR $8 AN HOUR ON A $9,000 COPIER THAT A $60 REPAIRMAN COMES TO FIX...

Panel 7: I FIELD A ZILLION CALLS FOR $8 AN HOUR KNOWING IT'S JUST A MATTER OF TIME BEFORE I'M REPLACED BY A $40,000 VOICE MAIL SYSTEM THAT A $75-AN-HOUR TECHNICIAN WILL INSTALL.

Panel 8: I'D SMASH MY HEAD AGAINST THE WALL, EXCEPT THE $40-AN-HOUR PLASTER REPAIRMAN WOULD HAVE TO COME OUT OF MY SALARY.

Panel 9: SLIMY CLIENTS... SNAKEY BOSS... UNKNOWN MONSTERS LURKING BENEATH THE SURFACE...

Panel 10: ...AND THE HARDER I TRY TO GET OUT, THE FURTHER I SINK INTO THE MUCK.

Panel 11: IT'S MORE THAN A SECRETARIAL POOL.

Panel 12: IT'S A SECRETARIAL SWAMP.

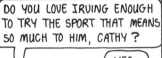

83

THIS SEASON ON TV THERE ARE WEDDINGS HAPPENING ON "L.A. LAW," "PERFECT STRANGERS," "CIVIL WARS," "WONDER YEARS," "BABY TALK," "HOMEFRONT," "GOLDEN GIRLS," "NORTHERN EXPOSURE," "A DIFFERENT WORLD," "BEVERLY HILLS 90210," "LIFE GOES ON" AND "CHEERS."

A LOVING TRIBUTE TO OUR RENEWED COMMITMENT TO DEEP, STABLE, NURTURING, LONG-TERM RELATIONSHIPS!

THIS SEASON IN REAL LIFE THERE ARE SPLIT-UPS HAPPENING FOR FERGIE AND ANDREW, PRINCESS ANNE AND MARK PHILLIPS, TAMMY FAYE AND JIM BAKKER, WINNIE AND NELSON MANDELA AND APPROXIMATELY 40% OF THE REST OF THE POPULATION WHO, BY ALL ACCOUNTS, WERE AS PERFECTLY MATCHED AS PEOPLE CAN GET.

MEN DON'T WATCH ENOUGH PRIME-TIME TELEVISION.

YOU CAN'T WEAR HIGH HEELS ON THE GOLF COURSE, CATHY.

PANTS WORN WITH FLATS MAKE MY LEGS LOOK FAT, IRVING.

WOMEN ARE SUPPOSED TO WEAR GOLF SHORTS!

I DON'T SEE YOU BARING YOUR LEGS IN SHORTS.

ONCE AGAIN, MEN GET TO PARTICIPATE IN AN EVENT WITHOUT EXPOSING ANYTHING PERSONAL! MEN WALTZ THROUGH LIFE WITH NO EMOTIONAL RISK WHATSOEVER!!

IT'S AN EMOTIONAL RISK TO BE IN THE SAME ROOM WITH YOU!!

I CAN'T WEAR SHORTS. MY PANTYHOSE ALL HAVE RUNS.

THOSE AREN'T THE GOLF SHORTS I GOT YOU, CATHY.

OH...AHEM... I HAD TO EXCHANGE THEM.

I GOT YOU A SIZE 5 JUST LIKE YOU SAID YOU WORE.

YES...AHEM... WELL... THEY WERE CUT A LITTLE FUNNY.

WHY WOULDN'T A SIZE 5 FIT IF YOU WEAR A SIZE 5?? YOU DO WEAR A SIZE 5, DON'T YOU?

DROP THE SUBJECT! LET'S PLAY GOLF! WHO'S FOR GOLF?!

...AND THEY THINK WE DON'T UNDERSTAND THEM...

CAREFUL WITH THOSE SUIT-CASES! YOU'LL BREAK YOUR BACK! CAREFUL WHERE YOU WALK! YOU'LL SLIP AND CRACK YOUR SKULL!

PUT ON YOUR HAT! YOU'LL CATCH PNEUMONIA! BUTTON YOUR COAT! YOU'LL CATCH YOUR DEATH! PUT ON YOUR GLOVES! YOUR FINGERS WILL FALL OFF!

HAVING SURVIVED 18 BUSINESS TRIPS, A DAILY FREEWAY COMMUTE, AND LIFE IN GENERAL FOR THE PAST 364 DAYS, A WOMAN FACES HER MOST TREACHEROUS JOURNEY YET...

...MAKING IT UP THE SIDEWALK TO HER MOTHER'S HOUSE.

DON'T WALK SO FAST! YOU'LL FALL AND POKE YOUR EYE OUT!

Guisewite

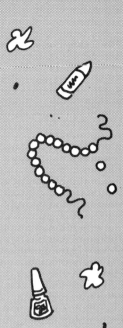

DOGS AREN'T ALLOWED IN OFFICES AND STORES. IT ISN'T CATHY'S FAULT. SHE FEELS TERRIBLE LEAVING ME. SHE'D TAKE ME IF SHE COULD.

IT ISN'T HER FAULT SHE WAS STUCK IN SOME HORRIBLE BUILDING WHERE THEY DON'T ALLOW DOGS!

I'M TOO TIRED TO PLAY, ELECTRA. I JUST SPENT FIVE HOURS CHASING A LITTLE BALL AROUND A 20-ACRE PARK.

ANOTHER DOG CROSSES THE FINE LINE BETWEEN KISSING AND SPITTING ON HER OWNER'S FACE.

...AND THEN ON THE THIRD HOLE, IRVING WAS ABOUT TO SWING AND HE....

...OH, NO. I CAN'T THINK ABOUT IRVING ANYMORE WITHOUT THINKING ABOUT GOLF!

HE SNEAKED THE GOLF GERM INTO MY BRAIN AND IT'S TAKING OVER MY WHOLE ROMANTIC CONSCIOUSNESS!! WHEN I IMAGINE HIS FACE, I THINK GOLF !!...I IMAGINE HIS ARMS... I THINK GOLF !!

GOLF GOLF GOLF GOLF AACK GOLF !!!

BEGINNERS ALWAYS GET SO OBSESSED WITH THE GAME.

I KNOW YOU'RE NOT HAPPY ABOUT IRVING AND THE GOLF THING, BUT WOMEN ALWAYS HAVE TO DO THE COMPROMISING IN RELATIONSHIPS, CATHY.

MY GENERATION DOES NOT BELIEVE IN COMPROMISING, MOM!

YOU MIGHT NOT BELIEVE IN COMPROMISING, BUT YOU STILL HAVE TO **DO** THE COMPROMISING.

WE DO **NOT** HAVE TO COMPROMISE!

WELL, YOU DON'T **HAVE** TO COMPROMISE, BUT IF **YOU** DON'T COMPROMISE, **NO ONE** WILL COMPROMISE AND THEN THERE WILL BE NO RELATIONSHIP, WHICH, OF COURSE, IS A VERY BIG COMPROMISE.

FUNNY HOW THE ONLY TIME I KNOW SHE'S LISTENING TO ME IS WHEN SHE'S NO LONGER SPEAKING TO ME.

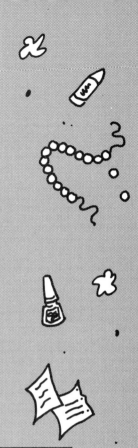

89

I SHOULD DO SOME WORK...
I SHOULD MAKE SOME CALLS...
I SHOULD PAY SOME BILLS...
I SHOULD DO SOME LAUNDRY...
I SHOULD CLEAN OR...OR...

...OR MAYBE I NEED A LITTLE SNACK.

YES! SNACK! A SNACK! GET UP FOR A SNACK!!

I DIDN'T EVEN MOVE!

I HEARD THE MENTAL WRAPPER OPENING.

TV SHOWS IN RERUNS...COMIC STRIPS IN RERUNS...SEQUELS TO MOVIES I DIDN'T WANT TO SEE IN THE FIRST PLACE...

ENTERTAINMENT

IS THERE NOT ENOUGH ORIGINAL THOUGHT TO SUSTAIN SOME BASE LEVEL OF NEW MATERIAL THROUGH THE SUMMER??

DOES THE AVERAGE WORKER NOT BEAR ENOUGH TEDIUM WITHOUT BEING REMINDED EVERY DAY THAT THE CREATORS OF OUR MEASLY ENTERTAINMENT ARE ON VACATION WHILE WE'RE STUCK WITH THEIR CRUMMY RERUNS??!

I'M SICK OF IT!! I AM SICK OF YOUR RERUNS!!

SHE SAYS THE EXACT SAME THING EVERY YEAR.

LIFE IMITATES LACK-OF-ART.

WHERE'S CHARLENE, CATHY?

CHARLENE'S NOT HERE ANYMORE, MR. PINKLEY.

WHAT DO YOU MEAN, SHE'S NOT HERE?

CHARLENE DOESN'T EXIST ANYMORE.

THE PERSON YOU KNEW AS CHARLENE HAS BEEN TRANSFORMED FROM A BRIGHT, DEDICATED PROFESSIONAL...

...TO A FINGER WITH A BODY ATTACHED.

I GOT A RING!! MY ENGAGEMENT IS OFFICIAL! I HAVE THE RING!!!

SIMON SURPRISED YOU WITH A RING, CHARLENE?!

NOT EXACTLY. I'VE BEEN WHINING ABOUT GETTING ONE SINCE LAST FEBRUARY.

HE SURPRISED YOU BY PICKING IT OUT?

NOT EXACTLY. I STUCK PICTURES ALL OVER HIS HOUSE OF THE ONE I WANTED.

HE SURPRISED YOU BY BUYING IT?

NOT EXACTLY. I DRAGGED HIM TO THE MALL AND STARTED WAILING AT THE TOP OF MY LUNGS OUTSIDE THE JEWELRY STORE.

HE SURPRISED HER BY NOT LEAVING TOWN IN DISGUST FOUR MONTHS AGO.

MEN CAN BE SO UNPREDICTABLE.

CHARLENE AND SIMON HAVE BEEN DATING A TENTH AS LONG AS WE HAVE AND THEY'RE ENGAGED, IRVING.

THAT'S NICE.

THEY'RE STREAKING TOWARD THE FINISH LINE AND WE'RE STILL STUCK IN THE FIRST LAP! ...THEY'RE AHEAD OF US!! EVERYONE IN THE WORLD IS AHEAD OF US!!

WE CAN STILL WIN, IRVING! WE HAD THE BEST START! WE HAVE TO RALLY! FOCUS! **GET OFF YOUR BUTT, MY DARLING, AND GO FOR ALL YOU'VE GOT!!**

ANOTHER RELATIONSHIP FALLS VICTIM TO THE OLYMPIC SPIRIT.

— CLICK —

MY FIANCÉ CAN GET A TUX IN 10 MINUTES! WHY DOES A WEDDING DRESS TAKE A YEAR?!

VERY SIMPLE.

Bridal Wear

BY APPOINTMENT ONLY

WHEN A MAN GETS MARRIED — BOOM-LIFE GOES ON... BUT WHEN A WOMAN GETS MARRIED, SHE HAS TO ALTER HER NAME, CAREER PATH, DOMESTIC SKILLS CLUTTER TOLERANCE AND PHONE TIME, NOT TO MENTION SPEND THE REST OF HER DAYS TRYING TO RECOUP THE BODY THAT WILL VANISH WITH BABY NO. 1.

IN SHORT, THE BRIDE'S LIFE REQUIRES 300 TIMES THE ALTERATIONS THAT THE GROOM'S DOES AND SO, SYMBOLICALLY, DOES HER DRESS!

BY APPOINTMENT ONLY

EVEN IF THEY DON'T HAVE IT WHEN THEY COME IN, BRIDES ALWAYS HAVE THAT SPECIAL GLOW WHEN THEY LEAVE.

Bridal Wear

BY APPOINTMENT ONLY

I NEED A SIMPLE WHITE COCKTAIL DRESS FOR MY WEDDING IN OCTOBER.

THIS IS AUGUST. THERE'S NO WHITE IN THE STORE.

HOW ABOUT WINTER WHITE?

NO WINTER WHITE. ALL WINTER CLOTHES COME OUT IN SUMMER, EXCEPT WINTER WHITE, WHICH WON'T BE OUT UNTIL SPRING.

I CAN SHOW YOU A COZY BLACK VELVET GOWN... A DRESSY WOOL SUIT... OR THE EVENING WEAR RAGE, A LONG CHIFFON SKIRT WITH A SHORT, KICKY JACKET.

"THE BRIDE WORE A TWEED SPORT-COAT."

IF YOU CAN HOLD OFF UNTIL THE JANUARY CRUISE-WEAR COMES IN, I CAN PUT YOU IN A NICE WHITE TERRY COVER-UP!

WHO'S JOAN AND WHY IS SHE ON OUR GUEST LIST, CHARLENE?

I GOT HER AN $85 FORK FOR HER WEDDING. SHE HAS TO COME TO MINE.

WHO'S BETH?

I GAVE HER A $130 VASE. SHE HAS TO COME.

I GAVE BARB A $55 FRAME... JANET A $73 CHAMPAGNE BUCKET... LISA A $120 WOK...

YOU DON'T EVEN **SPEAK** TO THESE PEOPLE ANY-MORE!! HOW CAN YOU IN-VITE THEM TO THE WEDDING?!

A WOMAN NEVER FORGETS THE VALUE OF FRIEND-SHIP.

WILL YOU GO SHOPPING FOR WEDDING CHINA WITH ME?

YOU WANT MY MOTHER TO GO SHOP-PING WITH YOU??

YOUR MOM GIVES SUCH GOOD ADVICE, CATHY!

YOU THINK MY MOM GIVES GOOD ADVICE??

SHE'S SO MUCH FUN!

YOU THINK MY MOM IS FUN??

WHY DON'T YOU ASK YOUR OWN MOM??

MY MOM? ARE YOU KIDDING?! HOO, BOY! MY MOM??!

MOTHERS ARE LIKE HEDGE CLIPPERS. NO ONE WANTS TO OWN THEM, BUT EVERYONE WANTS TO BORROW THEM.

Panel 1: THESE THINGS ARE ALL SO NICE, CHARLENE, BUT DUE TO THE HARD ECONOMIC TIMES, MANY BRIDES ARE SKIPPING THE FANCY SHOPS AND REGISTERING FOR WEDDING GIFTS AT A....

DON'T SAY IT! DON'T SAY IT!

Bridal Registry

Panel 2: I DON'T WANT TO HEAR THOSE WORDS! I'M SICK OF THOSE WORDS! I LIVE MY LIFE IN THOSE WORDS!!

Panel 3: I WILL NOT HAVE MY CHANCE FOR A BIG GIFT HAUL TAINTED WITH THOSE WORDS!!!

Panel 4: ...DISCOUNT STORE.

AAUGH!!

OH, GOOD. A TRADITIONALIST. SHALL WE BEGIN WITH THE $500 TOAST SERVER?

Bridal Registry

Panel 5: THIS IS A VERY POPULAR CHINA PATTERN!

NO. SIMON WOULDN'T LIKE THAT.

Bridal Registry

Panel 6: THAT'S TOO FRILLY FOR SIMON... TOO TRENDY FOR SIMON... TOO EARTHY FOR SIMON...

Panel 7: TOO ARTSY FOR SIMON... TOO STUFFY FOR SIMON... TOO SOUTHWESTY FOR SIMON... TOO MODERN FOR SIMON...

Panel 8: PERHAPS YOU SHOULD JUST BRING SIMON IN.

ARE YOU KIDDING? HE NEVER HAS AN OPINION ON THIS KIND OF STUFF!

Bridal Registry

Panel 9: CHARLENE AND SIMON ARE GETTING MARRIED. IT MAKES ME FEEL SO OLD, IRVING.

WHAT DO THEY HAVE TO DO WITH YOU, CATHY?

Panel 10: ANDREA AND LUKE ARE ABOUT TO HAVE THEIR SECOND BABY. IT MAKES ME FEEL SO OLD.

WHAT DO THEY HAVE TO DO WITH YOU?

Panel 11: MICK JAGGER IS A GRANDPA.

AAACK!!

Panel 12: I MAY BE OLD, BUT I STILL KNOW HOW TO GET A MAN MOVING.

BEFORE THE WEDDING, I'M GOING TO GET A DIFFERENT HAIRDO, DIFFERENT BODY, ALL NEW CLOTHES AND BECOME AN EXPERT IN GLOBAL POLITICS SO WE CAN HAVE FASCINATING DINNER CHATS!

THEN SIMON WON'T BE MARRYING THE PERSON HE DATED, CHARLENE.

ARE YOU KIDDING?? SIMON NEVER EVEN **DATED** THE PERSON HE DATED!

I HAVEN'T BEEN TOTALLY MYSELF WITH A MAN SINCE THE SECOND GRADE!

CAN YOU BELIEVE THAT, CATHY??

DON'T LOOK AT ME. I PEAKED IN KINDERGARTEN.

🎀 DIARY OF A BRIDE-TO-BE 🎀

DAY 1: GOT RING AND PLEDGED TO SHARE OUR LOVE, OUR HOPES, OUR DREAMS, OUR EVERYTHING FOREVER AND EVER AND EVER...

DAY 2: ATTEMPTED TO LEAVE A TOOTHBRUSH AT HIS HOUSE.

Diary of a Bride-to-Be

A DRAWER?? WE'RE ENGAGED TO BE MARRIED AND ALL I GET IS A MEASLY DRAWER??!

A DRAWER! SHE'S TAKING OVER MY HOUSE!! SHE HAS A WHOLE DRAWER!!

YOU'RE NOT MOVING IN FOR TWO MONTHS, CHARLENE! WHY ARE YOU ALREADY TRYING TO TAKE OVER MY WHOLE BATHROOM??

CUPBOARD SPACE IS SYMBOLIC OF EMOTIONAL SPACE, SIMON.

A PERSON WHO CAN'T GIVE UP MORE THAN ONE DINKY DRAWER IS A PERSON WHO CAN'T GIVE UP MORE THAN ONE DINKY PART OF HIS HEART!

IF I WERE MOVING INTO **YOUR** HOME, HOW MUCH OF YOUR CLOSET WOULD YOU GIVE ME?

MY CLOSET?? NONE! ARE YOU KIDDING?? NO ONE TOUCHES MY CLOSET!!

I REST MY CASE.

WHAT CASE?! YOU HAVE NO CASE!! ...AND IF YOU DO, I NEED IT FOR MY EXTRA MAKEUP!!

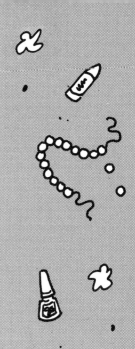

OF COURSE, ALL OUR BRIDE GOWNS TAKE A FULL YEAR TO ORDER.

I WAITED 35 YEARS TO MEET HIM...TWO YEARS FOR HIM TO USE THE WORD "US" IN A SENTENCE...

...TWO YEARS FOR HIM TO CHOKE OUT A PROPOSAL...AND SIX MONTHS FOR HIM TO MENTION THE SUBJECT AGAIN!! I AM NOT WAITING ANOTHER YEAR FOR YOU TO STICK A BUNCH OF SEQUINS ON SOME MOSQUITO NETTING!!!

I WANT A GOWN AND I WANT IT **NOW**!!!

MY NEXT APPOINTMENT TO SHOW DRESSES IS IN MID-NOVEMBER.

IS THERE AN EXPRESS LANE FOR THE OLDER BRIDE?

WE'RE HAVING A SMALL WEDDING.

FINE. THEN WE DON'T NEED TO THINK ABOUT CENTERPIECES.

WEDDING PLANNER

OH, NO! WE NEED CENTERPIECES! ENGRAVED PLACE CARDS! MONOGRAMMED RICE POUCHES, LIVE BAND, FULL BUFFET, ICE SCULPTURE, AND A FLOCK OF LOVE BIRDS RELEASED INTO THE AIR AS WE DASH INTO OUR WAITING LIMO!!!

WHICH ASPECT OF THE WEDDING WAS GOING TO BE SMALL?

THE GROOM QUIT SPEAKING TO HER YESTERDAY, SO YOU CAN CUT THE GUEST LIST BY ONE.

WEDDING

OUR NORMAL LEAD TIME IS FOUR MONTHS.

I PUT OFF MARRIAGE TO "PURSUE A CAREER".

Wedding Cakes

AFTER 18 YEARS OF SLAVING, THE ONLY THING I'VE ACHIEVED IS THE KNOWLEDGE THAT THERE ARE NOW 300 MILLION 25-YEAR-OLD WOMEN COMPETING FOR THE FOUR MEN MY AGE WHO ARE PARANOID ENOUGH ABOUT COMMITMENT TO STILL BE SINGLE!

IT'S A MIRACLE THAT I'M ENGAGED TO ONE, AND IF YOU CAN'T CRAM ANOTHER WEDDING CAKE INTO YOUR FALL SCHEDULE, I'M GOING TO MARCH INTO YOUR KITCHEN AND BAKE IT MYSELF!!!

RUN FOR YOUR LIFE!! IT'S ANOTHER "MATURE BRIDE"!!!

DON'T ANSWER THE PHONE, IRVING! IT MIGHT BE CHARLENE!

((RING RING))

IT MIGHT BE MOM ASKING ABOUT CHARLENE... IT MIGHT BE SIMON COMPLAINING ABOUT CHARLENE!

((RING RING))

EVER SINCE HER ENGAGEMENT, MY LIFE HAS BEEN CONSUMED BY CHARLENE! I NEED A NIGHT OFF FROM CHARLENE!

GREAT. WHAT DO YOU WANT TO DO?

LET'S TALK ABOUT CHARLENE.

OH, HOW MEN TREASURE THESE RARE INSIGHTS INTO THE MINDS OF WOMEN.

BEFORE SIMON, I SPENT MY PAYCHECK ON GOOFY CLOTHES TO ALLURE TOTAL LOSERS... ...MY MOTHER BOUGHT PASTRIES TO CONSOLE HERSELF.

I SPENT MY SAVINGS ON RIDICULOUS SHOES TO IMPRESS VARIOUS GEEKS...MY MOTHER BOUGHT CHEESECAKE AND CHOCOLATE TO CONSOLE HERSELF.

I CHARGED MY LAST DIME ON LUDICROUS GETUPS TO WOO MR. WRONG.... MY MOTHER BOUGHT VATS OF ICE CREAM TO CONSOLE HERSELF.

WHAT PREPARATIONS HAVE YOU MADE FOR THE WEDDING?

I'VE GIVEN MY TROUSSEAU TO THE GOODWILL, AND MY MOTHER HAS EATEN MY DOWRY.

A 25-YEAR-OLD BRIDE CAN EXPECT TO SPEND $15,000 ON HER WEDDING.

A 30-YEAR-OLD BRIDE WILL WANT TO ADD A FEW MORE ELEGANT TOUCHES.

AFTER AGE 35, OF COURSE, A BRIDE HAS THE SOPHISTICATION AND MEANS TO POP FOR THE FINEST OF EVERYTHING MONEY CAN BUY!

AFTER AGE 35, I SHOULD BE ABLE TO CHARGE ADMISSION!

HOW MUCH COMMISSION CAN I MAKE ON A WEALTH OF INDIGNANCE?

CAN WE AFFORD THE ORCHID BOUTONNIERES FOR THE USHERS?

NO.

CAN WE AFFORD THE SOLO HARPIST FOR THE RECEPTION?

NO.

ON YOUR CURRENT BUDGET YOU CAN AFFORD TO RIP PHOTOS OUT OF "BRIDE'S MAGAZINE", STICK THEM TO THE WALL OF YOUR GARAGE, AND HAND OUT POTATO CHIPS TO PASSERS-BY.

POTATO CHIPS ??!!

IT'S ALWAYS AN EXHILARATING MOMENT WHEN THE BRIDE FINALLY COMES TO TERMS WITH THE THEME FOR HER WEDDING.

I DID IT, SIMON !!! I FINALLY LINED UP A CHEAP PLACE FOR THE RECEPTION, FOUND SOMEONE WHO'LL BAKE A CAKE FOR $30, AND BEGGED A FRIEND TO TAKE PICTURES FOR FREE!

I'VE LEARNED TO LET GO... TO LIGHTEN UP... AND TO FOCUS ON WHAT REALLY MATTERS IN THIS WEDDING...

MY PARENTS JUST SENT A LIST OF 35 MORE PEOPLE THEY NEED TO INVITE.

...COMMITTING MURDER.

ALSO, MOM WANTS US TO MOVE THE DATE UP TWO DAYS.

DON'T WRITE LETTERS...check! DON'T LOSE WEIGHT...check! DON'T CLEAN CLOSETS...check!

DON'T ORGANIZE PHOTOS...check! DON'T SAVE MONEY...check! DON'T FALL IN LOVE...check! DON'T TRAIN DOG... check!

TA DA! IT'S NOT EVEN LABOR DAY AND FOR ONCE IT'S ALL CHECKED OFF!

IF AT FIRST YOU DON'T SUCCEED, REPHRASE THE LIST.

AFTER TWO OF THE WORST YEARS IN RETAIL HISTORY, WE'VE HEARD THE CALL AND RESPONDED WITH A WHOLE NEW CONCEPT IN FASHION!

OUT WITH LAST YEAR'S NATTY NATURAL FIBERS... IN WITH THIS YEAR'S ACRYLIC BLENDS!

OUT WITH LAST YEAR'S EARTH-TONE CAPE... IN WITH THIS YEAR'S RED LEATHER BOMBER! OUT WITH LAST YEAR'S FABRIC-SAVING MINI... IN WITH THIS YEAR'S 20-YARDS-OF-MATERIAL SUIT!

IN SHORT, FORGET THE PLANET!! SAVE THE MALL!!

MY SALESCLERK IS EXPERIENCING A MELTDOWN.

Row 1:

FALL, 1992! THE FASHION BUZZWORD IS "LANKY"! THE BUZZWORD IS "LONG"! THE BUZZWORD IS "LEAN"!

THE BUZZWORD IS "LANKY, LONG, LEAN, TALL, TOWERING, PENCIL-THIN SILHOUETTE"!!

5'2", 138 POUNDS.

SPLAT

SALESCLERK WITH A BUZZWORD MEETS CUSTOMER WITH A FLYSWATTER.

Row 2:

THE LONG SKIRT WILL LOOK FABULOUS WHEN IT'S SHORTENED TWO FEET!

DO YOU HAVE ANY PINS?

PINS?

EVERYTHING IN YOUR DEPARTMENT HAS TO BE ALTERED. YOU MUST HAVE PINS!

WAIT! I MIGHT HAVE A PIN IN THE BOTTOM OF MY PURSE!

YOU SPENT A FORTUNE LURING US BACK TO THE STORES! YOU COULDN'T POP FOR A 39¢ BOX OF PINS?!

CRAWL AROUND ON THE FLOOR! THERE ARE ALWAYS A FEW PINS STUCK IN THE CARPET!

THE NEW ELEGANCE...

NOTE HOW YOUR REAR STAYS COMPLETELY COVERED THIS YEAR!

Row 3:

$25 BILLION SPENT TRYING TO LOSE POUNDS...

$14 BILLION SPENT TRYING TO LOSE INCHES...

TWO DECADES OF DEPRIVATION, STARVATION AND SWEAT, AND THE MOST FIT GENERATION IN HISTORY SLIPS INTO THE SLEEKEST NEW LINE IN YEARS....

YOU NEED A HEAVIER-LOOKING FOOT.

ALSO, YOUR HAIR'S TOO SKINNY.

Panel 1: IF YOU DON'T HAVE THE PLATFORM PUMP, YOUR SHOES ARE ALL WRONG. / I OWN 23 PAIRS OF SHOES, AND THEY'RE ALL WRONG??

FALL '92

Panel 2: THE ONE THING I WAS **NOT** GOING TO SPEND MONEY ON THIS YEAR, AND THEY'RE **ALL WRONG??** ARE YOU OUT OF YOUR MIND?! HAVE YOU COMPLETELY LOST TOUCH WITH THE NEEDS OF THE HARD-WORKING AMERICAN WOMAN??

Panel 3:

Panel 4: BRING ON THE NEW PUMPS! MY SHOES ARE ALL WRONG!!!

SHOES

Panel 5: MEN HAVE ENJOYED THE SIMPLICITY OF THE PINSTRIPED SUIT FOR DECADES... AND NOW, SO CAN WOMEN!

Fashions

Panel 6: MEN CAN TOSS ON A CLASSIC PINSTRIPED SUIT AND BE READY FOR ANYTHING... AND NOW, SO CAN WOMEN!

Panel 7: OF COURSE, A WOMAN WILL WANT TO ADD THE MATCHING HOSE, MATCHING SHOE, MATCHING BAG, COORDINATING BAUBLES, CONTRASTING BELT, FLOWING SCARF, KICKY HAT, AND FRILLY UNDERWEAR... ...BUT THE PINSTRIPED SUIT IS FINALLY OURS!!

Panel 8: WE'VE COME SO FAR! / AND WE'VE DONE IT HAULING SO MANY SHOPPING BAGS.

Panel 9: WE REJECTED MENSWEAR TWO YEARS AGO BECAUSE WE DIDN'T WANT TO LOOK LIKE MEN. / WE WERE JUST TOO INSECURE TO EXUDE OUR TRUE WOMAN-LINESS.

Panel 10: ANYONE CAN LOOK LIKE A WOMAN IN A DRESS... BUT TO LOOK LIKE A WOMAN IN A MAN'S SUIT TAKES SOMETHING EXTRA!

Panel 11: IN FACT, THE EXTRA WOMAN-LINESS REQUIRED TO BE WOMANLY IN MENSWEAR MAKES A WOMAN MUCH MORE OF A WOMAN THAN IF SHE WERE WEARING WOMEN'S CLOTHES!

Panel 12: FASHION'S NEW ACCESSORY: THE SALESCLERK'S MOUTH. / NOTE THE DAINTY WAY SHE GRIPS MY MIDDLE!

THE PINSTRIPED SUIT.

THE CADET UNIFORM.

THE COWBOY OUTFIT.

THIS YEAR, EVEN IF YOU DON'T HAVE A MAN IN YOUR LIFE, YOU CAN HAVE SOMETHING THAT LOOKS AS IF IT BELONGS TO ONE HANGING IN YOUR CLOSET!

AAUGH!

...AND FOR THE TRULY PASSIONATE, THE TARZAN GET-UP!

THE LEOPARD! THE ZEBRA! THE CHEETAH!

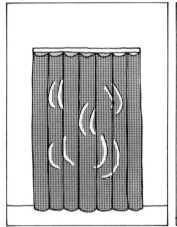

THE PIG.

I CAN'T WEAR A LEOPARD PRINT SUIT TO THE OFFICE.

NONSENSE. EVERYONE WILL BE WEARING THEM.

IF EVERYONE'S WEARING THEM, THEN I DEFINITELY CAN'T WEAR ONE TO THE OFFICE.

NOT TRUE. YOU JUST HAVE TO BE THE **FIRST** TO WEAR ONE TO THE OFFICE.

IF YOU'RE THE FIRST TO WEAR ONE TO THE OFFICE YOU'LL BE SETTING THE LEOPARD PRINT MODE, AND EVERYONE ELSE WILL JUST BE AN IMITATOR!

TA DA!

TOO LATE!

I WAS HERE FIRST! I WAS HIDING IN THE LADIES' ROOM!

PLUMMETING ECONOMY.
POLITICAL HOO-HA.
ROYALTY GONE AMUCK.

CRUMBLING HEROES.
CORRUPT MORALS.
ICKY AIR AND RAD VIBES.

AND ON TOP OF IT ALL, THE MASSIVE, COLLECTIVE CRANKINESS OF AN ENTIRE NATION IN WITHDRAWAL...

...FOUR MONTHS WITHOUT JOHNNY CARSON.

Sigh...

YOU'RE HOGGING THE COVERS.

WE WERE GOING ALONG FINE, AND THEN HE VEERED OFF IN A DIFFERENT DIRECTION.

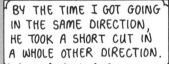

BY THE TIME I GOT GOING IN THE SAME DIRECTION, HE TOOK A SHORT CUT IN A WHOLE OTHER DIRECTION.

HE CUT... HE SWERVED... HE WOVE IN AND OUT... AND THEN HE WANTED TO KNOW WHY I WASN'T RIGHT THERE BY HIS SIDE WHEN HE FINALLY STOPPED LONG ENOUGH TO LOOK UP.

IF MEN INSIST ON TAKING THE RELATIONSHIP BACK-ROAD, WHY CAN'T THEY AT LEAST LEARN TO USE TURN SIGNALS?

ALTHOUGH MY BOSS COMPLETELY MISDIRECTED ME, I DISCOVERED A WAY TO BELIEVE I BLEW IT.

ALTHOUGH THE STORE WAS WRONG, I DISCOVERED A WAY TO TWIST THE FACTS SO IT COULD HAVE BEEN MY FAULT.

ALTHOUGH LAST WEEKEND WAS DESTROYED BY IRVING, I DISCOVERED A WAY TO BLAME MYSELF.

AND SO ENDS ANOTHER DAY FOR THE CHRISTOPHER COLUMBUS OF GUILT.

109

I TOLD MY MOTHER I WAS TOO BUSY TO TALK... AND THEN SPENT AN HOUR REHEARSING A MESSAGE TO LEAVE FOR A MAN WHO'S TOO BUSY TO SEE ME...

I BROUGHT HOME A BRIEFCASE FULL OF OVERDUE WORK AND BILLS...AND PROCEEDED TO ORDER $40 OF BUBBLE BATH FOR MYSELF FROM A CHRISTMAS GIFT CATALOG...

I THOUGHT THE LETTUCE LOOKED A TEENSY BIT WILTED AND MIGHT MAKE ME SICK... ...SO I ATE A HALF A ROLL OF COOKIE DOUGH FOR DINNER.

TO DO TOMORROW: THE OPPOSITE OF WHATEVER COMES NATURALLY.

I HAVEN'T HAD TIME TO READ THE PAPER... HAVEN'T HAD A CHANCE TO SEE THE NEWS...HAVEN'T EVEN GLANCED AT A MAGAZINE....

I'M BEHIND... HOPELESSLY BEHIND... REELING FURTHER BEHIND EVERY SECOND....

EVERYONE QUIT DOING THINGS UNTIL I HAVE A CHANCE TO CATCH UP!!

THE INFORMATION DECADE CLAIMS ANOTHER VICTIM.

HOO, BOY! HAVE YOU HAD THE RADIO ON THE PAST HOUR ??

GO AWAY.

....SO THEN IRVING GOT ANNOYED AND LEFT AND I LEFT THAT HORRIBLE MESSAGE ON HIS MACHINE...

...AND I WAS TOO UPSET TO DO THE PROJECT FOR THE CLIENT AND GOT IN SO MUCH TROUBLE AT WORK THAT I COULDN'T GET TO THE BANK AND THREE CHECKS BOUNCED AND....

...WHAT AM I DOING ?? YOU CAUGHT ME IN A WEAK MOMENT, MOM! I BLABBED TOO MUCH!! FORGET I SAID ANYTHING! PLEASE! FORGET EVERYTHING!!

ONE GOOD LUNCH: FOOD FOR A HUNDRED FUTURE CONFRONTATIONS.

I THOUGHT FOR WEEKS ABOUT WHAT I'D WEAR IF HE ASKED ME TO THE EVENT... WHEN HE CALLED AT THE LAST SECOND, I SAID I COULDN'T GET READY ON TIME.

I PLANNED A WHOLE AGENDA FOR A COZY WEEKEND AT HOME WITH HIM... WHEN HE WANTED TO GO FOR A SPONTANEOUS DRIVE, I COULDN'T COPE.

I FANTASIZED EVERY CONCEIVABLE ROMANTIC SCENARIO... WHEN HE KISSED ME AT THE TACO STAND, I DROPPED MY MEAL ON HIS FOOT.

SPLAT.

HOW CAN SOMEONE WHO'S SO READY FOR THE HOURS BE SO UNPREPARED FOR THE MOMENTS?

"PLANETS HAVE LINED UP TO MAKE THIS THE MOST PASSIONATE MONTH OF THE YEAR FOR HER him..."

ELLE

"SHE he WILL BE CONSUMED BY A DESIRE FOR TOGETHERNESS... AND WILL FIND HERSELF himself REACHING OUT WITH A FIERY NEW KIND OF NEED..."

ELLE

COME TO ME, MY DARLING!

DO YOU HAVE A FLASHLIGHT?? IT'S TOO DARK TO SEE ON THE GOLF COURSE!

THE DANGER OF INTERPRETING A MAN'S HOROSCOPE FROM A WOMEN'S MAGAZINE...

ELLE

I CAN'T HAVE A BRIDAL SHOWER FOR YOU THIS WEEK, CHARLENE. I'M HAVING A BABY SHOWER FOR ANDREA.

YOU NEVER EVEN SEE ANDREA ANYMORE, CATHY.

I NEVER SEE YOU ANYMORE, EITHER, CHARLENE.

YES, BUT I GOT TOO BUSY FOR YOU MORE RECENTLY THAN ANDREA GOT TOO BUSY FOR YOU!

THE LATEST PERSON TO DUMP YOU DESERVES TO HAVE A LAVISH PARTY THROWN FOR HER FIRST!

AH, THE ETHICS OF FEMALE FRIENDSHIPS...

ALSO, SINCE I'M MARRYING YOUR EX-BOYFRIEND, I SHOULD GET THE MORE EXPENSIVE GIFT!

I'M HAVING A JOINT BRIDAL AND BABY SHOWER FOR CHARLENE AND ANDREA, MOM, AND I...

SAY NO MORE, SWEETIE.

YOUR LAST SINGLE FRIEND IS GETTING MARRIED TO A MAN YOU ONCE DATED, AND THE FRIEND WHO TAUGHT YOU TO "PUT CAREER FIRST" IS HAVING HER SECOND BABY.

A SIMULTANEOUS MUTINY BY TWO DEAR FRIENDS WHO ARE MARCHING INTO HAPPY, NORMAL LIVES, LEAVING YOU ALL ALONE IN THE WRETCHED DEBRIS OF SINGLEHOOD. YES! I'LL BE THERE!! I'LL BE THERE FOR YOU, MY BABY!!

MOTHER, AS USUAL, WILL BE BRINGING THE PUNCH.

AN EVENING WITH WOMEN! IT'S BEEN SO LONG...DO YOU REMEMBER THE ENDLESS HOURS...THE LUXURY OF GETTING TO HANG OUT WITH WOMEN??

NO HUSBANDS...NO KIDS... JUST THE RICH, PROVOCATIVE COMPANY OF BRIGHT, INVOLVED WOMEN!

I'M ENGAGED. I'M SICK OF WOMEN.

I'M NOT ENGAGED. I'M EVEN SICKER OF WOMEN.

I HAVEN'T HAD A DATE IN TWO YEARS. I'M REPULSED BY WOMEN.

OH...IT'S ALL STARTING TO COME BACK.

WHO'S READY FOR A NICE BIG SLAB OF CAKE?

DO YOU HAVE ANY IDEA WHAT IT'S GOING TO BE, ANDREA?

IT'S A BOY. HIS NAME IS GUS.

HE'S BEING BORN BY C-SECTION AT 11:35AM OCTOBER 14, MAKING HIM A LIBRA WITH CAPRICORN RISING. HE'LL LOVE BOOKS, THE ARTS, HAVE A NATURAL AFFINITY FOR DEBATE, AND WILL PROBABLY GO INTO POLITICS.

HIS NUMEROLOGY AND SECOND-PLACE BIRTH ORDER INDICATE A COMPETITIVE SPIRIT, YET SENSITIVE DEMEANOR. HE'LL WEAR NEATLY PRESSED KHAKI SUITS, WILL MARRY AN EARTH SIGN, AND WILL BUY AMERICAN.

DOES HE HAVE ANY IDEA HIS MOTHER IS A LUNATIC?

OH, NO. WE WANT SOMETHING TO BE A SURPRISE!

I CAN'T BELIEVE IT, CATHY! IRVING'S STILL IN THE PICTURE ??

WELL...HE'S STILL DECIDING WHETHER OR NOT HE WANTS TO BE IN THE PICTURE.

I MEAN, HE NEVER OFFICIALLY SAID HE **WAS** IN THE PICTURE... ...BUT WHEN HE QUITS BEING IN THE PICTURE HE CAN'T STAND TO BE OUT OF THE PICTURE.

I THINK HE ONLY WANTS TO STAY IN THE PICTURE TO PREVENT SOMEONE ELSE FROM BEING IN THE PICTURE.

MY SWEETHEART: THE ROSS PEROT OF ROMANCE.

FOR CHARLENE, THE BRIDE-TO-BE, A PEEK-A-BOO NIGHTIE.

FOR ANDREA, THE MOTHER-TO-BE, A FLANNEL NURSING GOWN.

FOR CHARLENE, THE BRIDE-TO-BE, SCENTED MASSAGE OIL.

FOR ANDREA, THE MOTHER-TO-BE, DIAPER PAIL DEODORANT.

FOR CHARLENE, A LACE GARTER.

FOR ANDREA, A HEMORRHOID CUSHION.

FOR CHARLENE, A BUSTIER.

FOR ANDREA, A BREAST PUMP.

WOMANHOOD: A DIFFERENT HORMONE FOR EVERY GIFT CATEGORY.

I FEEL LIKE A GROSS WHALE. AN OBESE, EXPLODING COW.

I CAN'T BREATHE, CAN'T EAT, CAN'T SLEEP, CAN'T WALK. MY VITAL ORGANS ARE SQUASHED TO THE SIZE OF A PING-PONG BALL, AND MY HAIR IS FALLING OUT.

I HAVE HICCUPS, HEMORRHOIDS, HEARTBURN, VARICOSE VEINS, STRETCH MARKS, ITCHY EYES, NOSE BLEEDS, BLOTCHY SKIN, CONSTIPATION, LEG CRAMPS, AND BLOATED FEET.

I CAN'T WAIT UNTIL I GET PREGNANT!

NO ONE EVER LISTENS TO A MOTHER.

THE SHOWER WAS GREAT, CATHY, BUT I HAVE TO GET BACK TO THE LOVING ARMS OF MY FIANCÉ!

THE SHOWER WAS GREAT, CATHY, BUT I HAVE TO GO SNUGGLE UP WITH MY HUSBAND AND DAUGHTER BEFORE MY SON IS BORN!

THE SHOWER WAS GREAT, CATHY, BUT WE HAVE TO RUN HOME TO OUR BOYFRIENDS, HUSBANDS, KIDS AND/OR FABULOUSLY EXOTIC LIVES!

SHALL I PRETEND TO HELP YOU PUT AWAY THE REFRESHMENTS, OR SHOULD WE JUST SIT DOWN RIGHT HERE AND POLISH THEM OFF?

I WAS A GOAL-OBSESSED OVERACHIEVER WHEN MY FIRST BABY WAS BORN, BUT I'M GOING TO RELAX AND ENJOY MOTHERHOOD THIS TIME!

I WILL HAND-BUILD A CRADLE FROM KNOTTY PINE...STENCIL LITTLE FARM ANIMALS ON THE NURSERY WALLS...I'LL WEAR EARTH-TONE SMOCKS AND BIG STRAW HATS, AND I WILL KNIT!!

YES! MOMMY WILL KNIT THE LITTLE RECEIVING BLANKET THAT WILL CARRY HIM HOME FROM THE HOSPITAL!!

YOU GAVE BIRTH TWO HOURS AGO, ANDREA.

DON'T JUST STAND THERE! BUY MOMMY A KNITTING MACHINE!!

NO OFFENSE, BUT I DON'T WANT TO BE HERE WHEN THE DRUGS WEAR OFF.

QUICK, LUKE! HAND ME MY "TO DO IN THE HOSPITAL" BAG!

I JUST NEED TO FINISH A FEW THINGS FROM THE OFFICE... CATCH UP ON ALL MY READING AND CORRESPONDENCE...MAKE AN AFTER-SCHOOL SCHEDULE FOR ZENITH...AND PUT TOGETHER OUR WEDDING ALBUM FROM SIX YEARS AGO!

AT LAST! A FREE DAY!! ONE WHOLE DAY TO ORGANIZE MY LIFE SO I'LL BE FREE TO FOCUS ON OUR PRECIOUS NEW SON!!

MOST PEOPLE DON'T THINK OF RECUPERATING FROM A C-SECTION AS VACATION TIME, ANDREA.

A MOTHER LEARNS TO TAKE ANY DAY IN BED SHE CAN GET.

EAT HALF A POUND OF CHOCOLATE...

VALENTINE C·A·N·D·Y

♥CANDY♥

STRIP TO UNDERWEAR UNDER GLARING FLUORESCENT LIGHT. SQUASH WINTER-WHITE BODY INTO TINY PALE PINK CORSET...

VALENTINE L·I·N·G·E·R·I·E

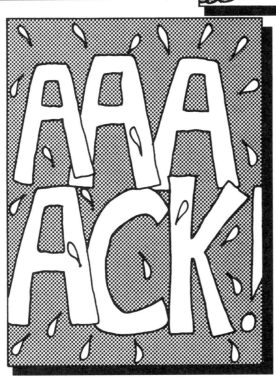

AAA ACK!

YOU CAN TURN OFF THE SURVEILLANCE CAMERAS. I DON'T THINK THERE WILL BE ANY BURGLARY ATTEMPTS TODAY.

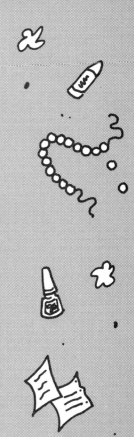

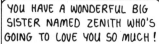

Panel 1: HI, GUS! I'M YOUR MOMMY! I'VE WAITED SO LONG TO MEET YOU!

Panel 2: YOU HAVE A WONDERFUL BIG SISTER NAMED ZENITH WHO'S GOING TO LOVE YOU SO MUCH!

Panel 3: YOUR DADDY IS HOME WITH HER RIGHT NOW, PLAY-ACTING THE MIRACLE OF BIRTH WITH THE LITTLE PREGNANCY DOLL GRANDMA SENT.

Panel 4: ...ZENITH?? HONEY?? WHAT HAVE YOU DONE WITH MOMMY'S TUMMY? FLUSH

Panel 5: ...WAIT! DADDY'S SETTING UP THE VIDEO! WE WANT TO CAPTURE THIS MOMENT FOREVER!

Panel 6: A BROTHER AND SISTER MEET FOR THE FIRST TIME.... THE FAMILY LIFE FORCE FUSED IN A PRECIOUS NEW BOND THAT WILL LAST FROM NOW UNTIL THE END OF TIME!...ROLL IT, HONEY!

Panel 7: WAAAH!!

Panel 8: CUT. IS IT ME, OR DO THEY ALREADY SORT OF RESEMBLE EACH OTHER?

Panel 9: CHANGE THE BABY... FEED THE BABY... PLAY WITH ZENITH... ROCK THE BABY... CHANGE THE BABY... FEED THE BABY... PLAY WITH ZENITH... CHANGE THE BABY...

Panel 10: I'M EXHAUSTED, BUT I MADE IT THROUGH THE DAY! I MADE IT, AND I SAVED JUST ENOUGH STRENGTH TO TUCK THE CHILDREN IN BED FOR THE NIGHT!

Panel 11: COME ALONG, CHILDREN! IT'S TIME FOR BED! IT'S 9:30 IN THE MORNING, ANDREA.

Panel 12: WAAH! WAAH!! WOULD THIS BE A BAD TIME TO MENTION THAT YOUR OFFICE HAS CALLED 20 TIMES?

THE CHILDREN ARE SLEEPING! ...THEY'RE BOTH SLEEPING AT ONCE! ...I NEED A SHOWER... I NEED A MEAL...I NEED A NAP...

I NEED FIVE MINUTES TO MY-SELF...JUST FIVE MINUTES TO SIT IN TOTAL SILENCE, COMPLETELY BY MYSEL—

RING! RING! RING!

...COME OVER?? YOU WANT TO COME OVER AND SEE THE BABY?? YES! COME OVER! WE'RE NOT DOING ANYTHING! HA, HA! BY ALL MEANS, COME OVER!!

THE NEED TO SHOW OFF SURPASSES ALL OTHER HUMAN INSTINCTS.

I JUST HAD A BABY. WHY AM I TRYING TO CLEAN THE HOUSE FOR COMPANY??

I JUST CREATED A HUMAN LIFE! WHY AM I TRYING TO FIND SOMETHING THAT WILL HIDE THE INCREDIBLE BODY THAT MADE IT POSSIBLE??

I AM REPULSED BY A WORLD THAT EXPECTS WOMEN TO CHEERFULLY BREEZE THROUGH ALL AREAS OF LIFE IN FULL MAKEUP! WHY AM I TRYING TO LOOK AS THOUGH NOTHING JUST HAPPENED???

GOODBYE, "WONDER WOMAN." HELLO, "WONDER-WHY WOMAN."

HI, ANDREA! YOU LOOK GREAT!

SHH! I DON'T WANT GUS TO HEAR THINGS LIKE THAT!

LIKE WHAT?

WHEN THE FIRST THING YOU MENTION IS HOW A WOMAN LOOKS, YOU PER-PETUATE THE FEEL-ING THAT LOOKS ARE ALL THAT COUNTS.

LITTLE GUS WILL NEVER GROW UP IN A WORLD WHERE MEN DON'T JUDGE WOMEN ON LOOKS IF WOMEN APPEAR TO BE DOING IT TO EACH OTHER! ...SHALL WE START OVER?

HI, ANDREA. YOU SEEM AS PREACHY AND OBSESSIVE AS EVER.

THANK YOU. YOU HAVE LIPSTICK ON YOUR TOOTH.

ZENITH WAS BORN IN THE '80s. WE WERE MATERIALISTIC, YUPPIE "SUPER PARENTS".

...BUT GUS IS OUR BABY OF THE '90s. NO NEWBORN FLASHCARDS... NO INFANT IQ TESTS... NO DESIGNER DIAPERS...

JUST THE SIMPLE, DOWN-TO-EARTH LIFESTYLE THAT, MORE AND MORE, DEFINES WHAT IT MEANS TO BE A FAMILY!

MOMMY AND DADDY ARE BROKE.

...ALSO, NOT SO MUCH EMPHASIS ON EARLY LANGUAGE DEVELOPMENT.

I WROTE A PRESENTATION THAT SAVED A MAJOR ACCOUNT THIS WEEK, MOM!

UM, HM.

I BALANCED MY CHECK-BOOK FOR THE FIRST TIME IN TWO YEARS!

UM, HM.

I WORKED OUT EVERY NIGHT AND LOST THREE POUNDS.

UM, HM.

OH, AND I VISITED ANDREA'S BABY.

YOU VISITED A BABY?? YOU WERE IN A ROOM WITH A BABY?? YOU HEARD BABY SOUNDS! YOU BREATHED BABY AIR!!

OUR DAUGHTER HAS HAD CONTACT WITH A BABY!!

...AND YET, WE START OVER EVERY WEEK WONDERING WHAT WILL MAKE THEM PROUD...

YOU WERE BORN IN THE YEAR OF FAMILY VALUES, GUS, AND MOMMY'S GOING TO RE-CORD ALL THE HAPPY, WHOLE-SOME SIGNS OF THE TIMES...

MOST POPULAR BOOK: 'Sex' by Madonna. MOST POPULAR SONG: 'Erotica' by Madonna. MOST POPULAR EVENT: Madonna topless at AIDS benefit. MOST POPULAR MAGAZINE: Madonna naked on cover.

RIP RIP RIP RIP RIP

DADDY WILL EXPLAIN WHY THERE'S NOTH-ING IN YOUR BABY BOOK.

WE'RE WAITING FOR SOME BETTER PICTURES.

119

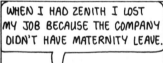

I'M WORKING HARDER WITH LESS TO SHOW FOR IT.

I HAVE CHILDREN I LOVE, A HUSBAND I ADORE, A JOB I NEED, AND A HIDEOUS FEELING THAT I'M FAILING AT ALL OF IT.

I NEVER FELT MY OPINION WAS SO IMPORTANT, AND NEVER HAD LESS TIME TO FIGURE OUT WHO AND WHAT REPRESENTS IT BEST.

ELECTION '92: YEAR OF THE EXHAUSTED WOMAN.

I THOUGHT MY LIFE WAS STRESSFUL UNTIL I SPENT AN EVENING WITH ANDREA'S DAUGHTER.

I THOUGHT MY JOB WAS IMPORTANT UNTIL I SAW HOW ANDREA'S SHAPED THIS LITTLE HUMAN BEING.

IN ONE BRIEF VISIT, EVERY SELF-RIGHTEOUS COMPLAINT OF MY LIFE GOT REDUCED TO SELF-INDULGENT DRIVEL.

JUST MY LUCK. I FOUND PERSPECTIVE, AND IT WAS HOLDING A BAG OF HALLOWEEN CANDY.

I'M SICK OF HEARING ABOUT IT... SICK OF READING ABOUT IT... SICK OF THINKING ABOUT IT...

...SICK OF EVERYONE'S OPINION ABOUT IT... SICK OF DISCUSSING HOW SICK EVERYONE IS OF DISCUSSING IT.

AND YET HERE I SIT, IN NAUSEATED FASCINATION, TO THE FINAL WRETCHED SECONDS.

JUST CALL ME A WOMAN WHO CAN'T LET GO OF A RELATIONSHIP.

Row 1

Panel 1: IN THE LAST ELECTION 39 MILLION WOMEN DIDN'T VOTE, BUT THIS YEAR'S PROJECTIONS ARE WAY UP.

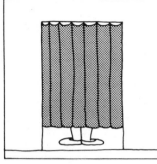

Panel 2: IS IT BECAUSE MORE WOMEN ARE WORKING? MORE WOMEN ARE WORKING MOTHERS? MORE OF THE ISSUES DIRECTLY IMPACT THE FAMILY?

Panel 3: OR IS IT BECAUSE, IN THESE STRESSFUL TIMES, THE ACT OF VOTING GIVES WOMEN SOMETHING THAT NOTHING ELSE IN LIFE CAN REPLACE...

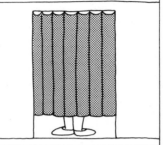

Panel 4: FIVE MINUTES TO MYSELF!!

WHAT TOOK SO LONG?

BALLOT BOX

Row 2

Panel 1: FOR MONTHS THIS OFFICE HAS BEEN DIVIDED BY THE ELECTION. THREE SELF-RIGHTEOUS CLIQUES POOH-POOHING THE OTHER SELF-RIGHTEOUS CLIQUES' POINTS OF VIEW.

PRODUCTIVITY

Panel 2: WELL, THE ELECTION IS OVER! IT'S TIME TO COME TOGETHER AS A COMPANY AND FOCUS ON THE ONE THING THAT MATTERS TO ALL OF US!

PRODUCTIVITY

Panel 3: MY WEDDING! MY PARKING SPACE! MY ALLERGIES! MY DOG! MY CHIP SHOT!

PRODUCTIVITY

Panel 4: RATS. THE INDIVIDUAL SPIRIT SURVIVED.

WE'RE A HEARTY BUNCH, MR. PINKLEY.

PRODUCTIVITY

Row 3

Panel 1: HI, SWEETIE. DID YOU NOTICE THAT CHICKEN FRYERS ARE ON SALE FOR 69¢ A POUND IN TODAY'S PAPER?

...WHAT? WHAT ARE YOU TALKING ABOUT??

Panel 2: THE MARKET HAS CHICKEN FRYERS FOR 69¢ A POUND TODAY!

MOM, I'M IN THE MIDDLE OF 12 PROJECTS AND HAVE TWO CLIENTS ON HOLD.

Panel 3: I WOULDN'T KNOW WHAT TO DO WITH A CHICKEN FRYER IF I HAD ONE, AND EVEN IF I DID, I WOULDN'T DROP $10,000 OF BUSINESS TO RUN ALL OVER TOWN SO I COULD SAVE 10¢ !! CHICKEN FRYERS! ARE YOU KIDDING ME ??!

Panel 4: SOMETIMES A MOTHER JUST LIKES TO MAKE SURE HER CHILDREN ARE THINKING ABOUT HER.

MY HOME: BOLTS ON WINDOWS. GUARD DOG ON DUTY. POLICE-MONITORED INTRUDER ALERT.

MY CAR: POWER LOCKS. MOTION-ACTIVATED ALARM. THEFT-PROOF HUBCAPS AND SOUND SYSTEM.

MY OFFICE: DOOR WIDE OPEN. EVERYTHING OUT ON DESK.

COME AND GET IT! TAKE IT AWAY! BURGLARS ARE WELCOME! YOO, HOO! IN HERE!!

FUNNY HOW UNDESIRABLE YOU BECOME WHEN THEY SENSE YOU'RE TOO AVAILABLE.

HAUL STUFF TO THE OFFICE. HAUL SAME STUFF HOME.

HAUL STUFF TO THE OFFICE. HAUL SAME STUFF HOME.

HAUL TO THE OFFICE. HAUL HOME. OFFICE. HOME. OFFICE. HOME. I NEVER DO IT. NEVER NEVER TOUCH IT. DON'T NEED IT. BUT HAVE TO HAVE IT WITH ME OR I FEEL LOST, DISORIENTED AND ALONE.

IS IT A BRIEFCASE, OR IS IT A BLANKEY?

BOOKS, CATALOGS, MAGAZINES AND NOTE CARDS IN CASE THERE'S NO TRAFFIC AND I GET TO WORK EARLY ENOUGH TO DO SOME PERSONAL THINGS...

MAKEUP IN CASE I GET INVITED TO A ROMANTIC LUNCH ... WORKOUT CLOTHES IN CASE I HAVE TIME TO STOP AT THE GYM ... VEGETABLES AND RICE-CAKES IN CASE I'M INSPIRED TO STAY ON MY DIET...

CASUAL OUTFIT, ACCESSORIES, KICKY LITTLE BOOTS, BLOW-DRYER AND HAIR SPRAY IN CASE I MEET SOMEONE CUTE AT THE GYM AND WE WANT TO POP OUT FOR A MOVIE...

WELL, IF IT ISN'T OUR LITTLE RAY OF HOPE AND HER FIVE-PIECE LUGGAGE SET!

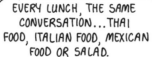

125

DIET PLANS IN EVERY PAPER, DIET ADS ON EVERY CHANNEL.

NAH... I'M NOT IN THE MOOD.

DIET FOOD ON EVERY SHELF IN THE STORE.

MAYBE SOME OTHER TIME.

A HUNDRED COMPANIES, A ZILLION PRODUCTS, ALL BEGGING TO HELP ME DIET.

HO-HUM... I'M NOT IMPRESSED.

THE ONE TIME IN MY LIFE I'VE SUCCEEDED AT BEING COY, AND IT'S BEEN TO AVOID LOSING WEIGHT.

WELL, WELL! THE MAROON SKIRT AND NAVY BLAZER!

ATTENTION ALL EMPLOYEES: CATHY'S WEARING THE **MAROON SKIRT AND NAVY BLAZER!!**

A HUNDRED ACCOMPLISHMENTS GO UNNOTICED, BUT THE ENTIRE COMPANY INSTANTLY RECOGNIZES MY "FAT CLOTHES".

MY LUNCH IS LOCKED IN THE TRUNK OF MY CAR SO I CAN'T EAT IT ON THE WAY TO WORK.

MY LUNCH HAS BEEN TRANSFERRED TO MY LOCKED BRIEFCASE SO I CAN'T EAT IT ON THE ELEVATOR.

MY LUNCH IS NOW BEING CARRIED TO THE COMPANY RE- FRIGERATOR, WHERE IT WILL REMAIN UNTIL PRECISELY...

...8:05 AM.

THIS OFFICE NEEDS SHORTER HALLWAYS.